Shadow Meal

Shadow Meal

Reflections on the Eucharist

Michael McNichols

WIPF & STOCK · Eugene, Oregon

SHADOW MEAL
Reflections on the Eucharist

Wipf & Stock
An Imprint of Wipf and Stock Publishers
199 W. 8th Ave., Suite 3
Eugene, OR 97401
www.wipfandstock.com

ISBN 13: 978-1-60899-360-4

Manufactured in the U.S.A.

Dedicated to my friends at St. Matthew Church, Orange, California, who have drawn me into their shared life and taught me to love the Eucharist.

And to the memory of Dr. Ray S. Anderson, who showed me that the table of the Lord is more expansive than I ever imagined.

Contents

Foreword

MIKE MCNICHOLS AND I are on the same eucharistic journey. He is well ahead of me, but this fine book has helped me to catch up a bit.

When I was growing up in evangelical environs we periodically celebrated the Lord's Supper—not very often, though. For some reason, we did not think it was important to do it frequently.

Indeed, for some Protestant folks, that attitude of only periodic communion services seems to be a matter of principle. I saw this once in a debate among some conservative Reformed types about the question of frequency. One person—arguing in favor of weekly communion—argued that by celebrating communion only six or seven times a year we were not following the example of John Calvin, who celebrated the Lord's Supper every week in his congregation in Geneva, Switzerland. This person's opponent, a defender of infrequency, responded that Calvin's congregation had services every day, but they had communion only on Sunday. This meant, he said, that Calvin celebrated the eucharist one service out of seven—so celebrating the Supper one Sunday every seven weeks seemed to be just about right for those of us who have services only one day a week!

The downplaying of the importance of the eucharist in my youth was reflected in the language we used. We "took communion" and the very idea of "taking" reinforced that notion that it was a take-it-or-leave it kind of event. Indeed, it was only when I got away from the "take communion" formulation that I began to change my understanding of the eucharist.

The shift in understanding happened for me when I was invited, in 1980, to a consultation focusing on a draft of a document, "Baptism, Eucharist and Ministry," that was officially adopted two years later by the World Council of Churches. In studying that document I was struck for the first time of the importance of the idea of the eucharist as a *meal*. This way of thinking about it helps us to get beyond the older debates about "real presence." Whether the bread and wine are mere symbols, or are somehow miraculously transformed into the "real" flesh and blood of Christ—those seem like less important questions when we agree that it is *the living Lord* who is really present as the Host of a meal to which he has invited us. That World Council document did not succeed in bringing Catholics and Protestants any closer to sharing the eucharist together, but it did bring *me* closer to a genuine love for coming to the Lord's Table.

The "meal" motif is highlighted throughout this book. More importantly, the eucharistic meal that we celebrate here and now is seen as pointing us to the greater banquet that we will share when we see our Host face to face in the coming Kingdom.

I am grateful to Mike McNichols for writing in such an inspiring way about the joys of eating and drinking together in the presence of the divine Host. In the best sense of the term, this is very much an "edifying" book. I can testify from personal experience that it stimulates the spiritual taste buds!

Richard J. Mouw

Prologue

The Bite of Eucharist

THERE IS A DISTURBING connection between the Eucharist and vampire lore.

On my trip home from Caracas, Venezuela, I sat next to a young woman on the plane who was an executive for a Hollywood film production company. We talked a little about the scripts she was reviewing, many of which sat piled in her lap. I suspect her heart was not in her work at the moment because we talked the entire time from Atlanta to Los Angeles.

She spoke intriguingly about a story that had recently caught her attention. It was a classy vampire novel and she was wrestling with the problem of turning it into a screenplay. There were certain problems to be solved in order to make the project work and she was stuck on a few of them.

At one point she explained to me that the legend of the vampire is the Eucharist turned backwards. Having read a number of vampire novels myself, I was able to affirm that this was the case. After talking together for about an hour, she asked me what I did for a living, and I confessed. I feared that, once she learned that I was (at that time) a pastor, the conversation would die and she would move to another seat or hide in the restroom. Instead, we spent the remainder of the flight talking about her life and her growing interest in God.

The Eucharistic part of our conversation sticks with me. In the Eucharist the body and blood of the one is given for the many. In the vampire story, the body and blood of the many are taken for the one.

All the thrills and villainy that I have enjoyed in the many vampire movies I've watched and stories I've read are no match for the puzzlement and obtuseness I've experienced in this mystery we call Eucharist, the

Lord's Supper, Communion. I wish I could say that the mystery is, for me, one of eternal shapings, but I must confess that it is more of a mystery of disconnection.

The Eucharist is something that confounds me.

A vampiric bite on the neck is supposed to bring death. I get that. A bite into the bread we call host is supposed to bring life. That, I do not get.

I'm not against the value and effect of the Lord's Supper, this bread and wine become body and blood. I am just befuddled by it.

I have two friends who have described a craving for Eucharist. They have times when they long for the taste of the bread on their tongue and in that they sense the presence of Jesus. I taste only bread and am thankful for the wine to wash it away. I appreciate the symbolism but I struggle with the presence.

This is, for me, a Eucharistic journey. I keep traveling to the table of Jesus, looking for the crumbs he might have left or the impressions of his elbows in the tablecloth. It's a regular process because Jesus continues to invite me. So I keep coming.

1

Lutheran Humiliation

I WAS BAPTIZED A Lutheran when I was four years old. I remember it clearly because it was one of the many times that I would cause my mother to wonder if she had scooped up the wrong baby at the hospital.

The Lutherans are sprinklers and I, in my little grey suit, was to be sprinkled one Sunday morning. There was a lovely baptismal font resting on a pedestal near the altar and I had to be lifted up to get the water somewhere near my head. I didn't know what this water ritual was really about but I was agreeable to it.

We were Lutherans because my father recoiled in horror at the prospect of attending a holy roller church, my mother's family tradition. My mother, never one to shy away from the opportunity for point-counterpoint, refused to go anywhere near a Catholic church, which my father, while not devout, would have preferred.

So they compromised by joining up for awhile with the Lutherans, who took us all in and then set about to sprinkle me in order to seal the deal.

Keep in mind that I was only four years old. I turned four in 1956, when Elvis was hot and preschools were not quite the rage. I was allowed to remain ignorant and blissful until kindergarten, which would come a full year later. So I was lifted to the font in all my uninformed glory.

The Lutherans must have known about my lack of knowledge, but they apparently didn't see the need to instruct me about what was going to happen. Somewhere along the way I must have had a premonition of my evangelical days yet-to-come, because I had the image of immersion in my mind. I didn't know how this would work, since the container holding the water appeared shallow. I looked at that wooden pedestal as I was lifted up on high and considered the possibility that it might be a vertical container and I was about to be inserted head first into a baptismal tube. I hoped they would not leave me there long since holding my breath under water was a new and unperfected skill. I prayed that my shoes wouldn't come off as they retrieved me from the murky depths. They were my new baptismal shoes.

I wanted to do this well, so when I saw my face reflected in the water, I was determined to offer my full cooperation to the baptismal process. Without urging or provocation I dunked my entire head into the basin, clunking my forehead on the shallow bottom. I raised my thoroughly soaked cranium up and out of the water, rivulets streaming down my grey baptismal suit. The pastor thought it was funny. My mother wanted to run screaming from the sanctuary. I was glad to have not drowned.

I suspect that this experience explains, in part, why I struggle with the profound nature of the Eucharist. Had I not humiliated my family on that baptismal Sunday in 1956, we might have stayed Lutherans and I would have been taught some proper things about the Lord's Supper. As it was, our history with the Lutherans was brief and, for the most part, uninstructive. I do not fault the Lutherans.

2

Necessary Symbol

When it comes to Christian traditions, Catholics, Episcopalians, Anglicans, and Lutherans have all the best stuff. Their clergy dress in robes and stoles. There are candles and crucifixes and crosses. Sometimes there is incense and an occasional statue or icon. When you walk into their church buildings, you know that something religious is afoot.

The remaining Protestant traditions are a little sparse on these things. The lack of such trappings is part reactionary and part theological. The reaction is to things linked to Catholicism, and it is against the Catholics that Protestants must, by definition, protest. Without the Catholics, Protestants would have nothing to protest, unless it would be themselves, which might not be a bad idea when you think about it.

The theological part has to do with avoiding things that might smack of idolatry and the conviction that God is encountered spiritually rather than through physical objects. So while many Protestant churches might be structurally appealing, they often avoid too many artifacts in order to keep the distinctions in tact.

There was not much consistent church attendance in my family during my pre-teen years, which was fine with me. In my view, a great way to louse up a weekend was to spend a fourth of it wearing a suit and enduring the unfathomable and unintelligible machinations of the Sunday service. My parents frequently fought over the topic of church and so we drifted through the ecclesiastical world as episodic Lutherans and momentary Presbyterians. None of it stuck with us.

When I was in fifth grade my parents considered sending me to a private Lutheran school at the same church where my immersion of humiliation took place. This was a disturbing shift for me, since I had been in the same elementary school since kindergarten. My public school was d one and my teachers, for the most part, were capable and

. Newman came to my rescue. She was my fifth grade teacher .dored her. She was strict, yet kind and creative. She summoned my parents to her classroom late one afternoon and convinced them to keep me in my public school. I never found out what happened in that meeting, so I don't know if Mrs. Newman was powerfully persuasive or if she had the goods on my folks and threatened to blackmail them for some dark, secret sin. Nevertheless, in one short meeting she won the day, very likely relieving my father of having to pay tuition for something that could be provided for free. From that day forward, I worshiped Mrs. Newman.

These were heady years for a kid my age. My schoolmates and I had gone through the Cuban Missile crisis together a year earlier, wondering why we needed to be at school if we were about to be blown to smithereens (I thought I could get blown to smithereens while watching TV and eating a Twinkie at home as effectively as I could while learning about California State History in school as the missiles whined overhead). John Glenn orbited the earth during my fifth grade year. Within twelve months President Kennedy would be assassinated and the Beatles would come to America to heal us of our grief. My teachers kept us attentive to world events and my school was a nutritious place for me.

Side-stepping the Lutheran school, however, also meant that I would continue to dodge the Eucharistic bullet. My public school would teach me about many things, but the Lord's Supper would not be one of them. The Lutherans almost rescued me, but Mrs. Newman's intervention trumped their missional passion.

Had I gone to the Lutheran school I would have also missed getting my brains beaten out over a girl when I was in sixth grade. The kid who hit me was considerably stronger than me and was wearing a large, steel ring on his slugging hand, which connected squarely with my skull. The girl kissed me on the cheek later as a reward for defending her honor, which had caused my attacker to pummel me into mush in the first place.

I missed Eucharist, but I was kissed for the first time. Some trade offs are tolerable.

~

Somehow my mother, probably through the use of hallucinogenic drugs and various forms of mind control, convinced my father to attend the local holy roller church. It was actually a church that had been birthed in the holiness tradition of the late nineteenth century, which meant absolutely nothing to me. All I knew is that we were at it again and I hoped that the phase would pass. It did not.

I was not hostile to God. I had an awareness of God and often prayed, particularly when I thought I was about to get pounded by someone, although sometimes, apparently, God didn't quite hear me. I was fine with God and I was pretty sure he liked me, but he clearly needed to do something about this whole church business.

Surprisingly, I found friends at this church. The people, while sometimes oddly vocal in their worship practices, were kind and welcoming (very undignified at times, but clearly entertaining and decidedly unLutheran). We still had to dress up, but it didn't seem so bad at this go-around.

Unlike the Lutheran clergy, these pastors wore suits instead of robes (they were, of course, all men). The sanctuary was lovely, but devoid of any symbols except a large cross behind the pulpit. There was no Jesus on this cross, unlike the Catholics who had some pretty graphic Jesuses on their crosses. The people were not necessarily anti-Catholic, but they were pretty sure that Catholic was the wrong road and would probably not take a person to heaven.

My dad and I did not buy into the bias against Catholics. My dad was not technically Catholic but had attended Catholic schools in the Midwest until high school. Many of my neighborhood friends were Catholic and I had even kissed a Catholic girl once. It was nice and convinced me of the worth and value of the Catholic race.

I learned in my new church that most religious things were symbolic. We did full-immersion baptisms but did not believe that the water actually did anything spiritual. We celebrated Eucharist (we called it Communion) once a month but did not believe that it did anything more than remind us of Jesus and his death 2,000 years ago. As I recall, those were the only things approximating sacraments that we did in our church.

At age sixteen I was baptized again. I was told that I needed to be baptized as a conscious, free-willed, clear-thinking Christian who was able to articulate his faith out loud and then get immersed in water symbolizing that I really meant it. As I look back, I wonder why anyone didn't point out the incompatibility between clear-thinking and the pubescent realities of the age of sixteen. Nevertheless, I did it and was glad to hear the people of my church affirm me in my declaration of faith in Jesus.

It seemed to me, however, that if these things were merely symbolic, then they were fundamentally unnecessary. It's not that they weren't important, but they weren't the real thing. Over time I came to see these rites as religious window dressing and didn't really care if I ever did them or not.

I think this ambivalence toward things symbolic has gone pretty deeply into my bones. I have neighbors who fly American flags in front of their houses. I understand that the flag is not my country, but merely a symbol of it. I do not understand why I need to purchase a flag and hang it off my roof when I am living in California. If I were living on the Moon I could see the point, but not when you live in a house that is on American soil.

Flying the flag also doesn't guarantee my patriotism. I spent four years in the Navy, for crying out loud. That should put a little shine on my American shoes. My neighbors can fly flags if they want and I'm okay with it. But it's symbolic and not the real thing. The real thing is the real thing.

Now, I'm not saying that I'm right about any of this. I'm just saying that this is how I've come to see things that are symbolic. In fact, I'm pretty sure I'm wrong about a great deal of it, but that's just how it is.

So when we took our monthly Communion, the symbolism just didn't go very deep for me. We were pretty somber and formal about the whole affair. Elders and church board members would line up at the altar at the front of the church and the pastors would hand out glittering trays of miniature shot glasses containing grape juice (we were holiness people, so wine did not touch our lips except late on Friday nights when one of my friends could scam a bottle of Spañada or Ripple[1]) and itty-bitty squares of crackers. These would then be passed down the rows and people would hold them until the pastor read the appropriate text of scripture. Then everyone would take, eat, for this was Jesus' body. Actually, it wasn't. It was all symbolic and, therefore, in my opinion, optional at best.

1. We were both Wesleyan and Arminian in our theology. Within that mix I learned that I could, and indeed did, lose my salvation repeatedly. Luckily, we had church services twice on Sunday and prayer meeting on Wednesday nights, so there were numerous opportunities to sin and repent, as long as the chorus of the hymn "Just As I Am" was sung enough times. With two services on a Sunday, you could do a lot of damage from Monday through Saturday, as long as it wasn't terminal. Then you were really in for it.

Even though we didn't believe that the bread and juice became the literal body and blood of Jesus, we were careful with the elements. And it's a good thing we didn't believe that because of what happened in our church many years later when Rhoda screamed.

Rhoda was an older woman who was a member of our church even though she considered it to be just a shade liberal for her tastes. She believed the cutting of a woman's hair to be scandalous and always wore long dresses and black, clunky shoes. She also, on occasion, got "The Blessing."

As a modified Lutheran, I had no place in my psyche for "The Blessing." I had become accustomed to the verbal affirmations ("Amen," "praise God," "hallelujah," etc.) that people would speak out during the pastor's sermon and after someone would sing a song for us. "The Blessing," however, was something else entirely. I learned that it was also called "having a spell." That seemed a little freaky to me, but as a lover of horror movies, I was intrigued.

"The Blessing" would occur when Rhoda felt that the Holy Spirit had cut her loose to emit a high-pitched, ear-splitting wail that could cause your back molars to crack in half. It would also scare the hell out of you, which is probably a good thing to have happen in church in the long run. It only happened once or twice when I was a teenager. It was some pretty great theater.

Some years later, after I got out of the Navy and finished college, I returned to that church with my wife and young daughters. I was soon on the church board and now eligible to serve communion to my fellow church members. I still didn't get it but was determined to take my responsibility seriously as a grown up Christian.

On one particular Sunday we were all lined up at the altar, having already served the congregation. The pastor had just handed us all our own little cups of juice and we were waiting while the organ played a quiet hymn. Standing next to me was our new youth pastor, a rather quiet young man who had never heard Rhoda share "The Blessing."

When most people yell or scream, they kind of work up to it, starting low and then moving toward a crescendo. Rhoda didn't bother with such preliminaries, but went right for high C. It was like getting hit square in the face with a water balloon that you didn't see coming. If she were a cowboy, her whoop would have rounded up every stray cow within a fifty mile radius of the church.

The Holy Spirit apparently decided to stir Rhoda up over some deep truth or revelation during our Communion service. When the force of her howl collided with the fine bones of our ears we all jumped until a little voice inside said, "Relax. It's just Rhoda having a spell." The new youth pastor, however, lacked such a still small voice and reacted as though someone had plugged him directly into a 220 outlet. Out of the corner of my eye I saw his body take on the form of a giant S and then snap back into something approximating uprightness. As he convulsed in terror, the contents of his Communion cup leaped into the air and splashed squarely on the altar.

It was a good thing that we didn't believe that this was really the blood of Jesus because now it was all over the place and no one would know what to do with that theologically. In addition, the sight of the youth pastor's spasms caused me to start laughing through my nose, which one should never do during Communion, symbolic or not. I began to vibrate, hoping that I would not also turn my body into an S and have to leave the premises.

Our youth pastor didn't last at our church very long, and I just couldn't blame him. Being the subject of someone's spell can be embarrassing.

~

During my Navy years Emily and I attended a church that the locals called "The Hippie Church." I loved that church and have always appreciated the investment that was made in my life during those years. On our first visit I saw the seats filled with a wild variety of people—young surfers still wet from the ocean, long-haired men and earth loving women, casually dressed 20-year-old men whose closely cut hair exposed their military attachment, and a small scattering of senior citizens. On that day, I knew I had found home.

This was not a church that was locked by tradition or a deep sense of history. It was 1974, the church was a year old and for many who had come to Christ during the Jesus Movement, Christianity was a relatively new phenomenon. We met in the multi-purpose room of an elementary school a block from the ocean, so even our physical space lacked ecclesiastical architecture. Since we met in a school, we had no symbols of the faith anywhere. That was fine with us, since we considered such religious symbols to unnecessary and even a distraction from what was real.

This church was of the mind that the Eucharist was also symbolic. I imagine we did it once in a while, but I'm at a loss to remember any specific occurrence. Yet we had a shared belief in the presence of God's Spirit among us and paid attention to that as often as we could. We would not have been concerned about the particularities of bread and wine or pita and grape juice. It was the thought that counted.

Some of our teenagers were gathered informally one night and got so excited about their faith that they decided to partake in an unplanned, spontaneous Eucharistic celebration. Since they lacked bread and wine, they used what was at hand: Pepsi and Fritos. After all, if it's just symbolic, then most anything will do. Any port in a storm, as they say.

3

Real Bread, Real Wine, Real Jesus

I HAVE A FRIEND who is Greek Orthodox. She is a skilled and passionate theological teacher and also knows her faith tradition inside and out. Her historical perspective on the church and why their traditions matter makes a low-church person like me feel like I've assumed that Christianity started immediately after Woodstock.

On occasion I am the guest homilist at a Catholic church that describes itself as ecumenical rather than Roman. I love worshiping with these fine people and they have embraced me as their token Protestant. They even allow me to partake in and serve the Eucharist, which is a bit daring in the presence of folks who have always been Catholic. The priest has assured his parishioners that it's okay, because I am ordained and, as a Protestant, I help put the E in Ecumenical.

When I serve at this church I wear an alb (robe) and a stole. Sometimes the stole is a bit long and drags slightly on the floor. While descending the altar one Sunday morning to serve the congregants, I stepped on the stole and stumbled, caused the wine I was transporting to slosh over the side of the chalice and onto the floor. My life passed before my eyes. I feared being shunned by my Catholic friends because of my clumsy handling of the blood of Jesus. I could hear echoes of Rhoda singing her spell into my brain.

To my great relief, my friend the priest merely turned to an acolyte and instructed her to wipe the wine up from the floor, and we carried on. No one seemed the worse for my error.

When I shared this story with my Greek Orthodox friend, she explained what would have happened in her church had the priest spilled the wine at the altar. He would, she declared, fall to the ground, press his face into the carpet and suck the wine out (I secretly hoped that Orthodox custodians were thorough in their pre-service vacuuming). After that, the violated section of carpet would be cut out and ceremoniously burned. That is a very different approach to the Eucharist than I have experienced. The Orthodox would probably not go for Pepsi and Fritos.

I am less challenged by the potential remedial actions of the priest than I am by the seriousness with which these people take the Eucharist. Either they value the Lord's Supper too much or I value it too little.

The Church has often, throughout its history, fought about the meaning of the Eucharist. Some have said that the bread and wine become the literal body and blood of Christ. Others say that the presence of Jesus is within the elements. Others, like my tribes, would say that it's all symbolism. We Christians seem to need something to fight about, and the Eucharist has often served as our line in the sand.

Taking things literally can be a problem. When my older daughter was a pre-schooler, my wife and I taught her some basic things about Christian faith. When we asked her the question, "Where is Jesus?" she would become somber, put her hand on her chest, and say with great reverence, "In my heart." Certainly, we reasoned, we have implanted a salvific concept into our four-year-old's life.

I studied child development in college and should have seen the folly of my ways. Four-year-olds don't do conceptual thinking very well. They are literalists. When we encouraged our daughter to "chew her food up," she would point her face to the ceiling and work her jaws with passion.

A prominent, retired minister in our church died soon after the passing of my grandfather. My little girl knew them both well and was troubled by their deaths. She came to me one day to inquire about their eternal destiny.

"Daddy," she said, "where is Pastor Burton?"

"He is with Jesus, sweetheart," I answered.

She stood silently for a while, pondering my glib response. Then her shoulders slumped and she appeared to have been weighted down with something heavy. I asked her why she looked so sad.

"Because now I have Jesus in my heart, I have grampa in my heart, and I have Pastor Burton in my heart."

Indeed. If these fine men are with Jesus, and if Jesus is in my tiny little daughter's heart, then there can't be much room left for future departees, let alone aortas and the like.

If bread and wine are body and blood, then they might be everything. If not, then they may be nothing.

Sorting out what this means has been a hazardous experience in the history of the church. When Jesus first started talking about body and blood, he lost voter confidence in a heartbeat.

> Jesus said to them, "Very truly, I tell you, unless you eat the flesh of the Son of Man and drink his blood, you have no life in you. Those who eat my flesh and drink my blood have eternal life, and I will raise them up on the last day; for my flesh is true food and my blood is true drink. Those who eat my flesh and drink my blood abide in me, and I in them. Just as the living Father sent me, and I live because of the Father, so whoever eats me will live because of me. This is the bread that came down from heaven, not like that which your ancestors ate, and they died. But the one who eats this bread will live for ever." He said these things while he was teaching in the synagogue at Capernaum.
>
> When many of his disciples heard it, they said, "This teaching is difficult; who can accept it?" But Jesus, being aware that his disciples were complaining about it, said to them, "Does this offend you? Then what if you were to see the Son of Man ascending to where he was before? It is the spirit that gives life; the flesh is useless. The words that I have spoken to you are spirit and life. But among you there are some who do not believe." For Jesus knew from the first who were the ones that did not believe, and who was the one that would betray him. And he said, "For this reason I have told you that no one can come to me unless it is granted by the Father."
>
> Because of this many of his disciples turned back and no longer went about with him. (John 6:53–66)

There are many hard things about following Jesus. Body and blood, it seems, are somewhere at the top of the list. It was a hard teaching then and it has been a hard teaching for 2,000 years. We've been eating body and drinking blood for a long time and we still can't completely agree on what it's all about.

Taking the Eucharist seriously as the body and blood of Christ is dangerous business. Early Christians were often under suspicion by a persecuting government because of rumors of cannibalism. *Eat my flesh and drink my blood.* It's a bit weird if you stop and think about it. I knew a man who, as a youngster, experienced the ecclesiastical danger of messing with the Eucharist. He told me that he was preparing the elements one Sunday morning while serving as an altar boy in his Roman Catholic church when his co-acolyte took a big slurp from the chalice. After licking his lips, this Eucharistic violator handed the cup over and very likely hissed like a snake and convinced his partner to do the same. *No one will ever know*, he whispered. *Don't be a chicken.* Caving into sin and the threat of the dreaded double-dog dare, my friend lifted the cup of Jesus to his lips and drank. As he looked over the top of the chalice he saw the priest storming directly toward him with a look of anger and reproach on his face. He knew that his life and eternal destiny now hanged in the balance, since the unauthorized blood of Jesus was in his stomach and on his lips. To his great relief, the priest merely suspended him from serving at the table for two weeks. It wasn't exactly purgatory but it got the point across.

Framing the Eucharist as purely symbolic is dangerous as well. It becomes too easy and may even lead me to believe that following Jesus and trusting my life to him is also easy. It is not. It has to do with death and resurrection, the carrying of a cross, participating in sufferings and loving a world that just might come to hate you. Symbols alone won't get me to do that.

Symbols don't have to be empty. They can create such a bond between their corresponding reality that violence and trauma ensue. The burning of a flag or the defaming of a cross are actions not taken lightly by the patriotic or the devout. If you spit on a photograph of my mother then you may as well have slapped her in the face. There will be hell to pay for that.

The ambassador of a nation is a symbol. As such, the ambassador represents the leader of that nation. When the ambassador of the US speaks, the president speaks. If the ambassador is held hostage, then the president may as well be held for ransom. The ambassador is no empty symbol. This symbol is about representation and it means something.

James and John, a.k.a. the sons of Zebedee, went to Jesus with a request that, if granted, would symbolize their respective places of importance in Jesus' retinue.

> "Teacher, we want you to do for us whatever we ask of you." And he said to them, "What is it you want me to do for you?" And they said to him, "Grant us to sit, one at your right hand and one at your left, in your glory." But Jesus said to them, "You do not know what you are asking. Are you able to drink the cup that I drink, or be baptized with the baptism that I am baptized with?" They replied, "We are able." Then Jesus said to them, "The cup that I drink you

> will drink; and with the baptism with which I am baptized, you will be baptized; but to sit at my right hand or at my left is not mine to grant, but it is for those for whom it has been prepared." (Mark 10:35–40)

When a person gets a job promotion, a new title, a corner office and all the trappings of authority, a change takes place. If that has ever happened to you then you know the feeling. All of those symbols change your perception of yourself and also cause others to see you in a new way. If I shift from being one of the rank and file workers to become vice president of whatever, my title becomes bigger than me. The office of VP changes me and draws me into a new world. While there might be false and even inappropriate identifications with titles and offices, the effect is real.

What might the spots to the right and left of Jesus symbolize for James and John? Very likely, they symbolized authority and maybe even power. The ones sitting to the right and left of a king get to whisper in his ear and speak privately about important matters that others may not hear. Such a symbolic promotion would change these boys and they didn't mind stepping up to the front of the line.

This, of course, made their companions upset. They might have been upset because of the audacity of the request or because they hadn't thought of it first.

Jesus is kind to them. I don't imagine they quite understood his response (I'm not sure that *I* do) because they too quickly claimed that they could drink his cup and share his baptism. Perhaps they saw these things as mere symbols—a literal cup of wine and a ritual dunking in the river—and figured they could do those simple acts as well as anyone.

Jesus' assurance that they will, indeed, drink his cup and share in his baptism has an ominous ring. The cup ends up being associated with his suffering and death (*remove this cup from me*) and the baptism, rather than symbolizing death, deals it out in spades. Jesus knows what he's talking about when he tells them they have no idea what they're asking. They are about to get in over their heads.

The positions of right and left, however, are a different deal. Jesus says he isn't able to grant that request because it isn't his to grant. This Jesus, who heals the sick, raises the dead, casts out demons and confounds the religious authorities can't make James and John his lieutenants. Why not? What's the big deal? He doesn't say they aren't capable of being good advisors or that they can't handle the authority. He just says it isn't his to grant. So whose is it to grant?

I've heard some say that Jesus is referring to his heavenly Father, that such positions in relation to Jesus are granted only by God. Maybe, but I don't think so. And I don't think the gospel writer Mark thought so either, because he offers up a twist to the story right towards the end:

> And with him they crucified two bandits, one on his right and one on his left. (Mark 15:27)

I suspect that Mark used a bit of ancient irony when he wrote this, allowing centuries of readers to connect the dots on their own. It appears that the positions to the right and left of Jesus were not symbolic, office-holding assignments. To the right and left of Jesus suffering and death happened that day. Jesus did not select his companions in death. It was not his to grant. Pontius Pilate took care of that. Those two bandits set the bar for future followers of Jesus. There's death in the air when *Just As I Am* is played on the organ.

When symbols become real they change us. When symbols are so closely tied to that which they represent that they draw us into new realities, then the disparity between symbol and actuality is insignificant. Symbols have power only when the real thing has power. The words "I love you" are written in the symbols of language, made up of letters that have no communicable meaning until they are expressed as authentic sentiment. The same words whispered in the ear by a lover can alter the course of a life even though the words themselves are only breathed symbols representing a deeper reality.

Bread and wine, consecrated or not, mean nothing without the reality of Jesus.

4

Don't Ask, Don't Tell

We religious people struggle with being either exclusive or silly. As much as I dislike exclusivity, I fear silliness more. I don't want to be silly and then convince myself that it's a good thing.

Exclusivism has its place. You may be a nice person, but you are excluded from my marriage to my wife. There's only room for two of us in our marriage and, while it might hurt your feelings or seem unfair or step on your right to do whatever in the world you want to do, you can't come in. This is clearly one of my hills to die on, and I'm pretty sure my wife feels the same way.

I am excluded from using the women's restroom in public places. And I want to clearly affirm how fine I am with that level of exclusivity. I also want women to be excluded from any restroom that I am currently using. We men are feral creatures and we generally choose to share certain things only among ourselves. I once unwittingly entered a unisex restroom in a London restaurant. As a woman emerged from the stall, I turned around and reported to my British friend that an unauthorized female was in the restroom to which I had been directed. He drew my attention to the unisex nature of the restroom and urged me to get over my American prudishness. I don't think I'm prudish, but I want the restroom hermetically sealed when I use it and limited only to the use of my fellow men.

There are some good reasons to restrict the inclusion of everyone in everything. Such restrictions often frame the Lord's Supper. Some churches allow only those who have been baptized to participate. Others want that baptism to be in their particular church. Some require particular church membership and still others expect the table to be approached by those who are freshly confessed and absolved.

This last restriction is particularly challenging for me. Once I've hocked up every sin that hovers at my consciousness and heartily sought

God's forgiveness, there are at least a couple of minutes before I actually partake in the elements. You have no idea what can happen in my brain in a very short period of time. My body might be able to move from confessional to table with observable penitence, but my mind can instantly be in a toga in Rio de Janeiro, dancing on a cocktail table with a red rose between my teeth. I think that counts for something and it probably isn't good.

I just don't like for anyone to be left out of something. When I was a kid my uncle Bernie gave me three valuable gold tokens that he had purchased at the Seattle World's Fair. I was thrilled and grateful, and promptly handed over two of them to my cousins Richie and Gary. My uncle looked at me like I was his nephew the idiot boy and just shook his head. He apparently wanted me to have those tokens to myself, even though he gave them to me right in front of my cousins. I couldn't imagine leaving them out.

It bothers me to be left out of the invitation to come to the table of Jesus and I don't want anyone else left out either. Paul the apostle, however, wanted to exclude some people from the Lord's Supper. He wanted to exclude the pigs, the ones who shoved their way to the front of the Eucharistic table and stuffed themselves sick while the poor among them went without (he writes about this in I Corinthians 11). Apparently the Corinthians had a much more substantial view of the Lord's Supper than we do, because most of us would starve even if we gobbled communion wafers all day long. Those crazy Corinthians. They got down and partied when it came to Eucharist.

The original Lord's Supper was exclusive in the sense that it only included Jesus and the twelve disciples. It's interesting that Judas made the cut since he was apparently up to no good. Jesus knew this, didn't he? I wonder why he let Judas in. A little exclusivism would have made sense to me if I were in charge of that dinner.

Of course, Jesus is the one who was given the nickname, "Friend of Sinners." Perhaps he let Judas in for the same reason that he kept having meals with tax collectors, prostitutes and other kinds of questionable life forms. There is a bit of a disconnection for me between *Jesus the Friend of Sinners* and *Jesus the Host of the Exclusive Table*. I know these exclusions are important to our churches; I'm just wondering if they are important to Jesus.

A friend and I once spent a few days at a beautiful Catholic retreat center as we planned a course we were going to teach. We discovered that retreatants could attend a special mass each morning, so we planned to show up. Since neither one of us were Roman Catholics, the mass intrigued us and, because we were both pastors, it seemed like a good thing for us to do. So, on our first morning, we wandered to the chapel right after breakfast.

The chapel was a new addition to the retreat center and sat on the edge of a hill, offering spectacular views of the surrounding countryside from its many windows. My friend and I were the only ones in the chapel and we killed time by inspecting all the fine points of the structure. After a while, we thought we had made an error because no one else showed up. There were plenty of other people at the center, mostly non-Catholics. Maybe they thought that mass didn't work for them because we only saw them at the omelet bar.

A door magically opened from the side of the chapel and a priest popped out, fully garbed in his clerical vestments. He was about our age and I noticed that he wore khaki trousers and running shoes under his attire. I liked him immediately. He graciously informed us that we would be meeting in the side chapel, and invited us to join him. Now there were three of us and we sat together in a small room with folding chairs all around the perimeter. At one end of the room was a small Plexiglas altar and podium. A candle burned on a little platform in front of the podium. On the podium was a large, open Bible while the altar held the elements of the Eucharist. He suggested we sit and get acquainted before we began the mass.

After we chatted for a while, my friend asked if we would be allowed to take communion. Actually, he was really asking if *I* could take communion, since my friend had been baptized as a Roman Catholic when he was a child. I considered this to be grossly unfair. It would be like traveling to another country with a companion and getting stopped at the border of the place you wanted to visit the most. As you turn away, your friend produces something that documents his dual citizenship and is allowed to pass while you are cast into outer darkness where there is wailing and gnashing of teeth. I was getting ready to wail and gnash.

The priest asked us, "Aren't you both Catholic?" We said we were not. He responded, "Oh. I thought you were priests." I have been mistaken for other things in my life, but this was a first. It occurred to me that we either carried a priestly vibe with us or Catholic priests, when out of uniform, could pass as Protestants just as easily. In fact, I felt flattered.

He thought for a moment, then said something to the effect of *operor non scisco, operor non dico*, which is roughly translated as *don't ask, don't tell.* We all laughed at that one. He went on to say that if the Pope can serve communion to the Episcopalian leader of Taizé right in the middle of St. Peter's square in Rome, then he could probably get away with it right here in this tiny chapel.

My friend and I were invited to read some of the Scripture texts for that day. Afterward, the priest said, "Let's talk about this awhile. I believe that the Holy Spirit speaks to us in community." So we did. We reflected together on the Scripture and considered how God might be speaking to us, to the church and to the world. Then he rose from his seat and read the Gospel text.

The priest then turned to the table and moved through the process of consecration of the elements. We sat obediently in our seats and waited. He then looked up at us and said, "Let's stand close together." So we got up and stood across from him at the table.

Body and blood, bread and wine. In the mouth, absorbed in the body. Zip. Gone. Presence of Jesus, transformed into Jesus, symbolic of Jesus—for me, just bread and wine. Except for this day.

In our brief time together we had become a community of faith. The priest—one middle-aged man among three—helped us to respond to the invitation of Jesus and then eat at his table. In that moment something happened for me. Bread and wine changed for me.

> *Take, eat; this is my body.*
>
> *Drink; for this is my blood.*

I began to believe it. I offer no theological explanation for this and can only report what I experienced. In that brief time and in that small, humble space, the Eucharist meant something to me. For me, the presence of Jesus was real.

The priest held out his hands to us and said, "Let's pray together." We clasped hands and prayed the Lord's Prayer—the Our Father. Then we sat down again and talked for a while before we exited the chapel and got on with our day.

I learned once that Dietrich Bonhoeffer had a notion about human relationships that helps me think about this experience. He said that in every combination of human relationships there is always one additional presence: The relationship itself. If two people are together in deep conversation, there is person A, person B, and the relationship that has formed between them, constituting entity C. If you've ever interrupted such a conversation you know about this. You realize quickly that there is a resistance to your presence because something else is already happening. If you join in, the whole thing dies and is resurrected as persons A, B, C, and entity D, the relationship.[1]

On that beautiful summer morning, I looked at my two spiritual companions and realized that something or someone else was present. Something tangible had been birthed—a society of Christian brothers, sharing body and blood, stories of life and hopes for the future. And in that small and fleeting society a fourth presence was apparent, the presence of Jesus bound up in the frail and temporal relationship of three middle-aged pilgrims.

It occurred to me later that this priest showed up every morning for mass whether or not anyone joined him. He prepared the elements, lit the candle, opened the Scriptures and waited. I'm sure that on many mornings, he sat alone. On our morning, he served God and his brothers, and taught me something about faithfulness.

Protestant services are often more like productions than gatherings for worship, even though I know that many are working to remedy that. In that morning mass I realized that the priest would not be concerned about the number of people that showed up or the size of the offering or whether the sound mix was good or whatever. Alone or with others, there would be Eucharist. Bread and wine would not be discarded. This was much more about the presence of Jesus than it was about anything else. It takes a faithful leader to come daily to that table under those circumstances.

I later told a friend of this experience and she scheduled her own retreat time at this center. She approached a different, older priest and asked if she could come to mass the next morning. He refused her, since she was not Catholic. She sadly returned to her room where she wailed and gnashed her teeth. Oh, well. Sometimes you are included, sometimes not.

I hope the priest who became my brother doesn't get in any trouble over this. If anyone ever asks me any further details about him, I will not answer. *Operor non scisco, operor non dico.*

1. Bonhoeffer writes about this in his book *Sanctorum Communio*, which was his doctoral dissertation, first published in 1930. For example: "The more the individual spirit develops, the more it plunges into the stream of objective spirit, and this immersion is precisely what strengthens the individual spirit" (74). He deals extensively with the human/divine relationships in chapter two.

5

Coffee Creamer Communion

As I have said, silliness is more fearsome than exclusivity for me. Exclusivity leaves me out; silliness makes me value things I shouldn't value.

For all the critiques my high-church friends offer about their own faith traditions, silliness is not generally among their complaints. What they do is fairly straightforward, well-practiced and grounded in their respective histories. Whether you like what they do or not, it is mostly not silly. In particular, Eucharist is not silly for them.

This might be due to the fact that the high-church traditions came to America from England and continental Europe. Those folks just aren't into silliness. Things would be a lot different if the first Pope had been from Pittsburgh or Des Moines or Los Angeles. Instead of bread and wine there might be whiskey and hot wings or lemonade and pretzels. In L.A., of course, it would have been green tea and tofu.

So, leave it to us to come up with Communion in a plastic coffee creamer cup.

I first encountered this at a pastors' conference a few years ago. Without any warning whatsoever, these little plastic containers were passed out to everyone. I didn't know what to do with mine. I take my coffee black so I didn't understand why I needed this until I noticed that the liquid contents of the cup were purple.

In this particular faith tradition, Communion is generally observed once a month or whenever someone remembers to schedule it. I was impressed, therefore, when it was announced that we would be sharing the Lord's Supper together, several hundred pastors and their spouses in a single room. And then the plastic flowed like living water.

This is actually a very ingenious invention, this body-and-blood-of-Jesus-in-a-handy-plastic-cup. One website brags on this "best-selling communion set" because of its economic use (you only use one per each person who actually showed up and save the rest for another time, probably in a month or two) and sanitary packaging (no longer dealing with the germ-ridden horrors of the common cup). Only in the U.S. would we meld pragmatism with Eucharist. It's a good thing there are a lot of Protestants in the U.S., otherwise there would be no profit in this at all. I don't think my Catholic friends would go for it.

When I first looked at the little purple cup, I wondered if the bread would come separately. Of course not! You simply peel the first layer of plastic from the top and you find the host (consecrated at the factory, no doubt), which you immediately gobble. Then you peel the second layer of plastic and you have access to the juice (not wine. With a large target market, you have to go with what pleases the majority of the potential customer base). It's easy, inexpensive, sanitary, private, and helps to keep our landfills stocked with plenty of non-biodegradable plastics with half-lives of a million years.

It's really a great idea because it allows me to remain isolated from my brothers and sisters and do this all by myself. I don't have to have the messy experience of kneeling side-by-side with people I need to forgive or those who need to forgive me. I don't need to stand on level ground with rich and poor, sick and healthy, sinner and saint. It's just me and the plastic-enshrouded elements, maybe with Jesus, maybe not. I don't know.

Maybe this is a fair trade with our Catholic friends. They invented the plastic dashboard Jesus and we invented the plastic Eucharist. It's a tragic trade off.

I suppose the plastic communion kit was inevitable in a consumer culture. Convenience is a significant value for people like us so we shouldn't be surprised that we decided to celebrate the Eucharist on our own terms. Are we thinking that Christians would end up refusing the body and blood of Jesus if we didn't offer it up on a plastic platter? We might be goofy and flawed, but I think we have more sense than that.

It is doubtful that Dietrich Bonhoeffer would like this one bit. If the presence of Jesus comes to us in the context of our human relationships, why is this utilitarian, individualistic approach to the Lord's Supper a good thing? For me, it's not that it is only symbolic; it's just plain silly. I won't do it anymore. If they serve me that again, I'm going out for coffee. No cream.

6

What is *This*?

As I read the Gospel accounts of the last supper I wonder how such a simple, highly relational meal became what it is today, either in its robust celebration or in its neglect. It was clearly a religious meal since it celebrated the Passover, the long-ago night before God rescued the ancient Hebrew people from their bondage in Egypt. The Passover meal symbolized the preparations for that great, redemptive event.

Matthew, Mark, and Luke are similar in their accounts of the Last Supper. This makes sense, since Matthew and Luke seem to have borrowed rather heavily from Mark. John, on the other hand, is a little sketchy on this topic. In John's account, Jesus gathers with his disciples before the Passover festival, and he does more foot-washing than he does eating.

Paul wraps the event up neatly for us when he gets after the Corinthians for all their shenanigans at the Lord's Supper.[1]

> For I received from the Lord what I also handed on to you, that the Lord Jesus on the night when he was betrayed took a loaf of bread, and when he had given thanks, he broke it and said, "This is my body that is for you. Do this in remembrance of me." In the same way he took the cup also, after supper, saying, "This cup is the new covenant in my blood. Do this, as often as you drink it, in remembrance of me." For as often as you eat this bread and drink the cup, you proclaim the Lord's death until he comes. (I Corinthians 11:23–26)

One thing appears consistent in the four Gospel accounts: All of this happened on the night that Jesus was betrayed. Paul quotes Jesus (we don't know the source of this quote) as saying twice, "Do this." I've sometimes wondered: What exactly is *this*?

1. Which may have been more of a "love feast," since it appears a full meal was offered. It still remains a marginal and fading practice today, known occasionally as a "potluck."

- Is *this* a ceremonial ritual?
- Is *this* a private meal with a few close friends?
- Is *this* a Passover feast, to be practiced only once a year?
- Is *this* a call to recognize and embrace the presence of Jesus in all the ordinary places, including each and every meal that nourishes our life?

Another big mystery of Christian faith is the incarnation, the *enfleshment* of God. Our creeds and theologies have wrestled repeatedly with what it means that the fullness of God was in Jesus the Christ, that God dwelt in him, that he was God-in-the-flesh, Emmanuel—God with us.

There is something incarnational about the last supper. There is food, harvested and raised from the earth, processed and prepared with human hands and ingested into bodies, sustaining and nourishing life. Jesus creates a link between these close-to-the-earth elements and his own body and blood. He engages in the meal with his friends. He offers his body and blood in symbol, and then offers it in actuality as he is snatched away through betrayal and conspiracy, isolated through fear and political power, abused in an effort to abstract him from the human community and crucified in order that the one might die so that the nation might live.[2]

In Jesus, God fully identifies with us. God can no longer remain abstract and unknowable to us once we've been encountered by Jesus. This Jesus consumed food and drink and invited others to join him. He broke bread and we would never again see it in an ordinary way. He would pass the cup and scandalously elevate its contents so that many would drink hearing him say, "This is my blood."

Jesus would show what happens when real people claim that the God of Abraham, Isaac, and Jacob is king rather than an emperor, a president, a congress or a body of religious leaders. He would accept the reality of betrayal, accusation, suffering, and death and do so as a real human being in real pain.

In Jesus, God fully identifies with us.

Jesus hangs on the cross and suddenly cries out, "My God, my God, why have you forsaken me?"[3] This cry has often been interpreted as Jesus

2. According to the high priest Caiaphas in John 11:50.

3. Matthew 27:46.

screaming out in terror as the God of Justice turns his back on the One who carries the vile sins of the world. But these words of Jesus are words that were given to Israel in Psalm 22:

> My God, my God, why have you forsaken me? Why are you so far from helping me, from the words of my groaning? O my God, I cry by day, but you do not answer; and by night, but find no rest. (vv. 1–2)

I hear Jesus crying the cry of Israel, a people in exile struggling to be the people of God and failing at every turn. I hear Jesus, hovering between life and death, offering his identification with the suffering and sense of abandonment of his own people. His death is then the ultimate in human identification as he experiences what all humans will experience as the inevitable consequence of birth. Throughout the story of Jesus we see God identifying with us.

And I am invited to eat at the table of Jesus. So are you, and so are the suffering, the dying, the marginalized, the sinner and the sinned against, the lovely and the unlovable. Jesus identifies with all and we are invited.

7

Identifying with Jesus

THE TWO MOST SIGNIFICANT sacraments in Christianity, baptism and Eucharist, are often linked to the idea of death. In baptism, we disappear under the water,[1] symbolizing our dying to sin. If all goes well and if the baptizer is skilled, then we also rise out of the water, symbolizing a spiritual resurrection into new life. In Eucharist, we take bread and wine in order to proclaim his death until he comes. Both sacraments carry a message of death.

I have to wonder, however, if the focus on death is more our interpretation of these sacraments than what is really embedded in the deep structure of these faith expressions. In western culture we tend to think judicially about our faith, and the death of Jesus becomes the means for human beings to find forgiveness from God. There might be something to that way of thinking, but I think there is more to it all than that.

When John baptized Jesus, they had an interesting yet somewhat cryptic exchange:

> Then Jesus came from Galilee to John at the Jordan, to be baptized by him. John would have prevented him, saying, "I need to be baptized by you, and do you come to me?' But Jesus answered him, 'Let it be so now; for it is proper for us in this way to fulfill all righteousness." (Matthew 3:13–15)

What was it about "righteousness" that needed to be fulfilled? The baptism of John was all about repentance. John was as shocked as we might be at the thought that Jesus had to repent of anything at all. But Jesus persists and John dunks him in the river. What was so righteous about that?

And what about ingesting bread and wine, given by the hand of Jesus to his conflicted disciples? What else could be going on except that this

1. If you do immersion. Sprinkling just doesn't seem death-like, does it? It's more like getting rained on.

last meal was a precursor to Jesus' death? Perhaps, at the deep core of these sacraments is identity: God, in and through Jesus fully identifies with us in our brokenness and sin. We, in our repeated revisiting of these events, identify ourselves with Jesus.

God's righteousness is a righteousness of grace. God puts all that is wrong in the world right by giving all of himself to us. When Jesus was baptized, he willingly identified with all human beings and their need for forgiveness and to be freed from the captivity of sin. When he served the bread and wine, he not only identified himself with God's rescue of the ancient Israelites from Egypt, but shared that meal with his disciples, identifying himself with them as friends.

Baptism and Eucharist are sometimes portrayed as being about us. More importantly, I believe, they are only about us to the extent that they are about Jesus.

~

Not too long ago there was a lot of hooplah in the media about whether or not retailers should allow their employees to wish people "Merry Christmas" during the Christmas season. The concern was that there might be some who did not observe Christmas as a religious season and their preferences needed to be respected.

One early-morning L.A. talk show host took exception to this debate. He loudly declared his disdain regarding the issue, claiming that since it clearly was the Christmas season, there should be no concern about discrimination or disrespect by merely saying "Merry Christmas." He thought the whole thing was ridiculous.

As I listened on my way to my office, I heard him turn from his microphone and call out to one of the station's young technicians, asking him to share a story with the audience. It went something like this:

"When I was a kid, my parents took me to this thing called 'The Glory of Christmas' at the Crystal Cathedral in Orange County. I was really excited about going and I was amazed when we got there. I saw all kinds of decorations, and animals walking around the stage and all kinds of great stuff.

"But in middle of the show, I got really mad. It wasn't about Christmas at all. It was about Jesus!"

The host of the show and his partner laughed heartily at the irony of the young man's story. I was glad for their laughter.

8

You Had Me at Unworthy

WHEN I PLANTED THE church that I led for ten years, I hadn't given much thought to the Eucharist. I assumed we would share communion the way our sending church and its tradition did it: Monthly (maybe), in plastic cups with French bread in baggies. It didn't much matter to me.

One of the members approached me one day and said, "I think the Lord wants us to do communion every week." He said things like that once in a while, but not in a freaky I-know-God-and-you-don't sort of way. I once saw him tell a young man he didn't know that God was waiting for an RSVP. The young man went pale, and I knew why. His friends had been sharing their life of faith with him and he was keeping God at arm's length. That next week he trusted his life to Jesus.

So when this member told me what he thought God's preferences were for our practice of the Eucharist, I paid attention. I decided he was right and I set about to bring a little more dignity to the practice. I got better plates for the bread and cool little ceramic cups for the wine and an antique-looking bowl for juice, just in case there were people who needed that (we had some recovering alcoholics in our midst and they struggled with the idea of sipping even a little wine, blood of Jesus or not).

But I had yet to deal with the question: Who can join in? My distaste for things exclusive could allow me to take all kinds of unevaluated liberties, so I worked on fleshing out my theology of the Eucharist.[1]

I understand what a slippery slope this can be. If everyone just worked up their own theologies about things (which people do all the time), we'd be in a big mess (which we usually are). At the same time, I

1. I am indebted to Dr. Ray Anderson and his courses on Systematic Theology at Fuller Theological Seminary for helping me think this through.

wasn't convinced that just because we put certain boundaries around the communion table that we were resting in a safe harbor.

I struggled with the character of the Jesus I had come to know through Scripture. This Jesus turned the religious community on its ear by spending time with people at the margins of respectability, health, and ethnic purity. He intervened in the stoning of an adulterous woman before she even had a chance to repent for her crime.[2] He told a story about a heart-broken father racing out to receive a wayward son before the son could even spill out his well-rehearsed plea for mercy, and then ordered a fatted calf to be prepared for a welcome-home dinner. I had a difficult time reconciling this Jesus with a single text from the Apostle Paul that said,

> Whoever, therefore, eats the bread or drinks the cup of the Lord in an unworthy manner will be answerable for the body and blood of the Lord. Examine yourselves, and only then eat of the bread and drink of the cup. For all who eat and drink without discerning the body, eat and drink judgment against themselves. (I Corinthians 11:27–29)

I heard this same Paul claim,

> God proves his love for us in that while we still were sinners, Christ died for us. (Romans 5:8)

As I read Paul's critique of the Corinthians, it appears that being "unworthy" had to do with hogging all the food at the love feast and shoving their way to the front of the buffet line, causing the poor among them to go without eating. This had, it seems, more to do with disregarding fellow humans than it did with spiritual status. This Jesus who died for us when we were truly unworthy couldn't, I reasoned, be turning us away from his table until we became worthy. The Jesus of the Gospels didn't do things that way.

I was brought back to the "this" of I Corinthians 11:23–26 ("Do *this* in remembrance of me"). It seemed to me that the "this" was, more than anything else, our response to the invitation of Jesus to come to his table. The Eucharist became, for me, a joyous response of the most unworthy of all people to come to the table and dine with the Son of God.

2. Yes, I know that most scholars suspect that this text was a later addition to the Gospel of John, but the church throughout the ages has apparently considered it an important and consistent enough portrayal of the character of Jesus that it was never edited out.

I've heard that Suzanna Wesley, John and Charles's mother, came to faith in Jesus at the Communion table. I've also heard that Solomon Stoddard, Jonathan Edwards's father-in-law, invited the seekers in his colonial church to give their lives to Jesus as they came forward for bread and wine. So, I could be wrong about all this, but at least I'm in good company.

I've had some experiences, however, that have brought some comfort and confirmation to my decision to practice an open table when I was a pastor.

One Sunday the parents of one of our members were in town and, as was their usual custom, they worshipped in our church. They had been members of a mainline denomination for many years and they had become friends of our congregation through their periodic visits. On that day I offered a brief teaching about the Eucharist as I had come to see it, and we all gathered to take, eat, and drink.

At the end of the service the wife came up to me with tears running down her face. She grasped my hands in hers and said, "I just need you to know that Bill took communion this morning."

I thought to myself: *I know I'm supposed to be picking up on something, but pretty much everyone here took communion this morning.*

She must have seen the puzzlement on my face, because she went on to explain. "We've been members of our church for over forty years, and this is first time that Bill has taken communion."

I didn't understand. Their church was sacramental in nature and the Eucharist was celebrated every week.

"Why," I asked, "has he never taken communion before today?"

"Because," she said, "before today, he has never felt he was worthy."

The table of Jesus. Friend of Sinners. *Come to me, all you . . .*

Sometime later I was invited to participate in a weekend retreat that involved some seasoned Christians, a few new Christians, and some who were standing at the margins of faith, interested but hesitant to step in. My friend, who was leading the retreat, asked me to lead the communion service, recognizing that she and I shared an "open table" theology. I was happy to oblige.

I'm pretty good at containing my emotions. Some surely think that it's because I have intimacy issues or a fear of vulnerability[3], but I really

3. Which might be true, but I'd rather not talk about it.

think it has more to do with my discomfort in having fluids leak out of my eyes and nose in public. I also can't talk and cry at the same time like some seasoned revival speakers I have known. So you can imagine my surprise at what happened next.

I stood before the group and framed the Eucharist as the invitation to the table of Jesus. I went on to describe that table as I imagined it: Lined with countless chairs, laid out like a banquet feast, a place reserved for all people, and stretching out through eternity.

At that moment I caught a glimpse of something: Broken-hearted, wounded, rebellious people edging hesitantly toward the table, stunned by the realization that their names were already printed on little cards, always waiting for them to come and dine. I knew some of the stories in that room, and I saw those people shaking off chains of unworthiness and standing in the astonished recognition that God had always been calling them home.

And I lost it. I didn't see it coming.

I couldn't breathe, let alone talk. My wife, Emily, was there, wondering if I was having a heart attack. The graciousness and expansiveness of God's love overwhelmed me and I couldn't speak. There were others weeping in the room, and after awhile, we wiped our eyes and shared body and blood.

I believe that, while I was a sinner, Christ died for me. And in that act of sacrifice, God showed his love. I believe that Jesus invites me to *this*, his table, and I repeatedly drag my damaged, unloveable, unworthy self to a seat reserved for me as Jesus puts his arms around me and asks, "How about a bit of fatted calf? I've cooked it up just for you."

9

A Dangerous Table

SHAME AND UNWORTHINESS ARE hideous first cousins. They both serve to keep people out of places they'd like to be. They keep people isolated and create a caste system that keeps the privileged and the unclean in separate quarters. That might work for first class and coach, but it doesn't work in the community of Jesus.

For four years my church met in the smelliest building in town. On Saturday nights the place was rented out to groups that consumed more beer in one night than is produced in all of Milwaukee in a year. Most of it went inside human beings but a great deal also landed on the carpeted floor. The late-night custodian made a half-hearted effort to make things ready for our worship service, but even with our early morning effort, the place smelled pretty raw.

It was also a dumpy place, even through we tried to spruce things up a bit. We were a fairly casual bunch, so we didn't need things to be fancy and we even dressed in a pretty relaxed way to match our surroundings. One of the interesting results of this situation was that some homeless and disadvantaged people found it easy to engage with our church. Most of our homeless friends came every week (except for the one who was in and out of jail a lot). One woman came to us from a shelter for battered women.[1] Several were members of the Al-Anon club that met across the alley from our meeting place.

One day I had an idea: What if we threw a party for the people at Al-Anon? It would be a big dinner with no agenda other than to bless and encourage these folks. I ran the idea past the people in my church

1. The first day she showed up, she had no front teeth because someone had bashed them out. The day she arrived at church with a brand new set of white, shining teeth, we had a celebration as she flashed her new smile to everyone.

and they went for it. Our plan was to host the dinner in December, just before Christmas.

People took on the responsibility of creating a menu and folks volunteered to cook hams and sweet potatoes and all sorts of covered dishes. Three other guys and I put together a little rock 'n roll band for the purpose of entertainment (because we were all men, we called ourselves *The TestosterTones*, which I thought was pretty clever). One of our members who was also involved in Al-Anon volunteered to distribute invitations.

As the day grew closer, it occurred to me that no one might show up. We could be doing this for absolutely no reason. The people at Al-Anon came and went and we didn't even know if the invitations were making their way into the hands of the people. I kept my reservations to myself and we continued to prepare.

On the evening of our event the tables were set, the food was laid out and the band was tuned up and ready to go. Just as I was beginning to despair (which takes me about 20 seconds beyond my expectations), the main doors opened and forty people from Al-Anon poured in. We welcomed them, showed them to their seats, poured iced tea and coffee and did some rock 'n roll.

I had briefed the people of our church ahead of time that it was important to mingle with our visitors. Sometimes people in churches forget how frightening and lonely it can be to visit a place where everyone seems connected except for you. So we planned to both serve and share the meal we had prepared for our guests.

The food was magnificent and the conversation lively. Our band took a break and we joined in the feast. I sat next to a man named Patrick. His drinking had cost him a great deal in his life, but he had a responsible job and was working hard to pull things back together. In the midst of our conversation he turned to me and said something I will never forget.

"I think we all really appreciate this," he said, "but we don't understand why you would do it."

I wasn't sure what he meant. "Do you mean why we would host a dinner for people?"

"No," he said. "We don't understand why people like you would want to be with people like us. You guys are the good guys. We're the ones who have screwed up."

A combined feeling of horror and shame poured through me. That we, the church, could somehow be viewed as a place for the privileged and respectable made me ill. I looked around the room at the people in my church whose stories I knew: The one who committed a horrendous crime as a drug dependent youth; the ones who had been adulterers and then found forgiveness and reconciliation; the ones who used to make money selling drugs and now devoted themselves to God and their new families.

I said to Patrick, "We don't see it that way at all. As we see it, there is no *you* and *us*. There is only *us* together, people beloved by God."

Patrick looked stunned by my words. "I've never thought of that before," he said.

I found out later that this conversation had been repeated numerous times during the evening. *Why would people like you want to be with people like us?*

We want to do that because Jesus invites us to *this*, his table, and in doing so we remember him.

At the common table we are not only identified with Jesus, but also with one another. None of our qualifications or differences matter once we respond to the invitation of Jesus. Identifying our lives with Jesus sometimes feels easy for us, as long as we keep things abstract. Identifying with one another is where things get particularly messy because we find out how much brokenness we have in common.

Tom came faithfully to our church within the first year of its founding. Tom was legally blind and had to walk to his job every day, and on the way he would pass by a park where homeless people gathered. Tom loved Jesus and was fearless in his confidence in God's love, so he made friends with these folks and brought them to church. One woman who came on a regular basis was Deborah.

Deborah's life was in ruins. The first time she visited I couldn't tell if she was male or female. She had just come off a two-week alcohol and methamphetamine binge and looked like she was three blinks away from death. Tom said that she lived on the streets and slept anywhere she could throw her filthy sleeping bag. But she kept showing up and, as she sobered up, we got acquainted.

The following Christmas fell on a Monday, so we had church on Christmas Eve morning. Protestant churches are a little funny about the quirkiness of the calendar because it allows Christmas to move around a bit. Since it's very inconvenient for a holiday that celebrates the birth of Jesus to fall on a Sunday when worship and fellowship interferes with opening presents, attendance at church can be a little ragged. When Christmas Eve is on a Sunday, it's a little better. People show up for church but they generally take off quickly because there is celebrating to be done: Cozy fires, great food, generous gifts, love all around. I knew that in a few hours we would be with my wife's family and we would have our own celebration.

Then my eyes landed on Deborah, sitting in church with all the others. I asked Tom where she would be that night, and he confirmed that she would be out on the streets somewhere. So I quickly conferred with my board members and explained the situation to them. They readily agreed that we should pay for her to have several days in a hotel. I told Tom and he said he knew just the place. So he and I let Deborah know what we were going to do for her. She was pleased.

When our Christmas Eve service concluded, my board members disappeared with their families and I was left with the task of getting Deborah set up for the night. So Tom, Deborah and I made our way to the hotel, which was fine under the circumstances, but you'd never go there on vacation. It was on a street where many of the city's homeless population wandered about and I felt just a touch out of place there. When we arrived, the front desk of the hotel (a very generous word to describe this place) was closed because the person in charge had gone to lunch and wouldn't be back for an hour. So we decided to wander down the street to get some food.

Down the sidewalk we went, Deborah pushing her bicycle loaded with her worldly possessions, Tom hanging on my arm because he couldn't see where we were going. Street people passed us by, offering greetings to Deborah. I knew we had homeless people in our city, but I had no idea that this community of urban nomads experienced this level of interconnectivity until that day. We approached the corner and waited for the light to change.

As we waited, a car load of teenagers sailed by us. One of the kids leaned out the window and shouted something at us, offering a group insult to three homeless people wandering the streets. Three homeless people: Deborah, Tom and me. Merry Christmas.

At first I was offended and angry, and then it struck me: I've been identified with the people that Jesus loves. Jesus has summoned me here because he was already standing on the side of Deborah, identifying with her in her pain and alienation. And now I was being identified with her.

Over hamburgers I was introduced to another homeless man who knew both Tom and Deborah. We shook hands and talked together while his earlobes, shredded by years of piercings, flapped in the breeze of the overhead fans. He shared with us his own despair over his inability to quit drinking. He knew it was killing him, but he said that he just couldn't stop. As he left us, we wished him the blessings of Christmas and he wished them back to us.

The table of Jesus is a dangerous place. It rips out our categories and won't allow any self-created statuses or disqualifications to keep us from sitting together at the places Jesus has set for us. When the wine is served, we might be asked to show our ID cards. There is a photo of Jesus on all of them.

10

Re-Membering

I'M NOT MUCH OF a joiner. I resist the boundaries that define me as something of which I am a member. Membership may have its privileges but it also has its constrictions and has a tendency to caricaturize and stereotype people. Membership can also lure me into a false sense of security when I see my connection to the thing I've joined as the best way to view the world around me.

I am a member of one of the two major U.S. political parties, but I never tell people which one since I think they both stink. I don't like the labels created by either side and I don't want to be stereotyped by virtue of my membership. I have been an official church member (where there is a process of joining, a certificate, etc.) but I've been more drawn to churches where membership happens as you continue to show up and share your life. I'm not against membership, I just think it has its limitations.

I have an appreciation for the many Christian traditions that abound in the world. I am sorry when they circle the wagons and declare that they've got the goods on God and then come to the conclusion that everyone else is barking up the wrong theological tree. I've read websites that condemn to the smoky fires of hell all who do not believe rightly, particularly including the fifteen or twenty key points of doctrine shown on their "What We Believe" page. It seems to me that if getting your theological facts straight is the surest road to heaven then we're all in a mess of trouble.

Christian traditions, with all their craziness, have a richness of heritage in there somewhere. I wish we could appreciate that about one another a little more than we do. Rather than seeing these traditions as historic points in history that must be preserved at all costs, I think it would be great if we could see them as catapults into an uncertain future. I wonder what would happen if we mined (not uncritically) the heritages bequeathed to us by Augustine, Aquinas, Luther, Calvin, Wesley, Zwingli, Simons, Knox, Fox, Seymour, and the rest of that great cloud of witnesses, and then spread the wealth around. We wouldn't have to deconstruct or syncretize our traditions, but we might all be enriched by sharing such contributions.

Richard Mouw of Fuller Theological Seminary once shared an out-loud thought at a seminar I attended a few years ago. He said he thought it would be helpful if our Protestant denominations could see themselves in a way that was similar to how the Roman Catholic church viewed their various orders—Franciscans, Dominicans, Jesuits, and the like. The Catholics see these orders as groups within the same family that contribute in unique ways. Dr. Mouw hoped that we might one day see our denominations in a similar way. I wish for that as well.

I am an unofficial Catholic. I am the token Protestant minister at an Ecumenical Catholic Church in Southern California. While I am not always there (I attend another church with my wife), I deliver the homily on occasion and have been invited to teach some classes there. These fine people have welcomed me in, although I think they might have been suspicious of my non-Catholic nature at first. Now they treat me like their ecclesiastical cousin and offer their love and friendship when I show up.

This little church is another place where Eucharist has been meaningful for me. I not only can partake there (they offer an open table) but can also serve there (as clergy, I am invited to serve alongside a priest). When my friend, Father Peter, looks into my eyes and says, "Michael, the body of Christ, broken for you," I believe it. When I look at each parishioner and say, "The blood of Christ, shed for you," and see the look in their eyes, I believe it again. It is there that I understand how many view the Eucharist as a mystery.

This church has taught me to appreciate the representative symbols of their tradition. I love how they celebrate the mass with all the accoutrements and artifacts of their Catholic heritage. At the same time, I love how they recognize that Jesus is at the center of all this. Their friendship and liturgies have brought healing into my life.

A few years ago I was struggling with a change in my vocational life and was feeling very low about some transitions that were coming. On my way to a meeting related to these transitions, I received a voice message on my cell phone from Father Peter. He said,

"You know, Michael, it's Ash Wednesday today, and I'm pretty sure your church isn't doing an Ash Wednesday service. Why don't you come to ours at noon today?"

He was right. We didn't have an Ash Wednesday service at my church. I am ashamed to say that I didn't even remember that it was Ash Wednesday until Peter called. My meeting was scheduled for 11:00 AM so I didn't think I could make it in time for the service. However, the meeting wrapped up at 11:45 and I was only 10 minutes away from the church. The meeting had been interesting and not negative in any way, but the nature of it had left me feeling old and sidelined. Through no one's fault I felt like God no longer had much use for me. As I walked to my car, I had a sudden desire to be at that Ash Wednesday service. I showed up to the mass right at noon.

I was among twenty or so people who had taken the time off to attend. The mass was peaceful and sweet. Peter's homily was short, rich, and penetrating. It spoke to my heart and I cried real tears. I followed the other faithful Catholics to the altar to receive the ashen mark of the cross on my forehead. I wore it on my head all day so that everyone would know how sad I was. I was pathetic.

But I was also being healed. Some events emerged over the next few weeks that reminded me of God's care and love for me. I might have been getting old (it happens when you don't have the good sense to die young), but I had not been sidelined. I had asked God to show me the next step in my life and he was faithful to do that. My Catholic friends mentored me along that process without even knowing it.

In the mass, unlike in my more familiar Protestant services, the liturgy and symbols remind me who I am through things auditory, visual, tactile, and relational. When I pay attention to what is going on, I start remembering Jesus and I am then remembered. I remember with my mind, but I am re-membered by Jesus, drawn back into the reality that I am a member of his body, not by certification or qualification, but because he has summoned me into his life. I may not be a joiner, but I am a member.

In body and blood, in ash and tears, I am re-membered.

God remembers us.

being a part

11

Eucharistic Chainsaw

> Whoever, therefore, eats the bread or drinks the cup of the Lord in an unworthy manner will be answerable for the body and blood of the Lord. Examine yourselves, and only then eat of the bread and drink of the cup. For all who eat and drink without discerning the body, eat and drink judgment against themselves. For this reason many of you are weak and ill, and some have died. But if we judged ourselves, we would not be judged. But when we are judged by the Lord, we are disciplined so that we may not be condemned along with the world. (I Corinthians 11:27–32)

Paul the apostle suggests here that distorting the Lord's Supper has led some of the people into sickness and death. I confess that I do not understand that. I've seen plenty of people distort something about Christian faith (especially when they're on TV) and they seem to fare about as well as the next person. If you get hoggy about the Lord's Supper, does it turn into poison? Is this a dark reversal of transubstantiation—instead of bread and wine turning into body and blood it turns into anthrax and hemlock?

There is something a bit scary about all of this. The way that low-church people can't quite shake off the Eucharist and the way high-church people revere it suggests that it continues to loom largely in our corporate consciousness. The Lord's Supper seems as wedded to us as the daily dinner bell, and maybe without it we get sick and die. Having once tasted, we're hooked. If religion is the opium of we the people, then maybe Eucharist is our heroin. If you mess with it, the withdrawals could kill you.

A woman came to faith in Jesus in my church one Palm Sunday. She had been a hardened, angry atheist and God seemed to have grabbed a hold of her and shaken her until her teeth rattled. I liked her immediately—her honesty, her intellect, her voracious hunger to learn about and grow in this

God she had so stridently resisted. Our conversations about faith were stirring and robust. It seems that she intended to make up for lost time and get to know this cosmic Lover who had pursued her for so long.

One Sunday I invited her to assist in serving the Communion elements. I often had people from the congregation help me with that. She somewhat reluctantly agreed and I attributed her reluctance to her relative unfamiliarity with the communion process. When the time came, she stood up front with the other servers, holding both bread and wine. As people approached her, I saw that she began to tremble, and then shake. This was not one of those Pentecostal-type shakings that come under the power of the Holy Spirit. This was a shaking of terror. I realized that she was frightened of the body and blood she held in her own hands, offering up the life of the One she had once despised. Yet, here she was, taken in by Jesus' family and invited to his table, not only to partake but to also pass the plates to other hungry, thirsty brothers and sisters.

I feared that I might have unintentionally put her in harm's way by letting her help. What if she keeled over and died? I would be at fault. God would have killed her and I would have loaded his gun.

But I realized that this wasn't going to happen. God wasn't planning to kill anyone over these humble elements. This woman didn't come to the table any more or less unworthy than the rest of us. We all came broken and doubtful, damaged and frightened. We came because Jesus sent out the invitations and we showed up. She was overwhelmed by grace. That will shake you up every time.

I dearly love my two-year-old grandson, Jack. But I would never trust him with a chainsaw. He's a great kid, but a chainsaw in his hands would result in severed limbs and untold pain and heartbreak. Chainsaws are best left in the hands of the lumberjacks who know how to use them.

I think judgment is like that. Judgment is something that we human beings throw around like cheap Frisbees. We don't really know what judgment is, when you get right down to it.

Some equate judgment with condemnation. When that happens people are either really happy that they are in the judgment seat rather than in the place of being judged, or they are scandalized because no one has the right to judge anyone else and we should all just mind our own business and live in peace. I don't think either one of those concepts has anything to do with judgment.

Perhaps a more helpful way to think about judgment is in terms of discernment. Discernment is about selecting the best out of a set of options. Someone with a discerning palate makes a judgment about the better wine or the choicest food. When a judge and jury come to a decision about a legal case and pass judgment, they are coming to a conclusion about what has been discerned about something that has taken place. It's a process of sorting out what is right from what isn't right; it's about identifying what is true versus what is false.

Judgment, left in human hands, can become a dangerous weapon. It's dangerous when we use it for the purpose of harming or caricaturizing other people and it's dangerous when it reveals the dark parts of ourselves. The second danger, when grasped and processed, can actually be helpful.

Paul's declaration of judgment to the early Christians in Corinth is about identifying what they have revealed about themselves through their own actions. They have celebrated the Lord's Supper as a shared meal but have allowed the poor among them to go without food and drink. As a result, they have judged who they really are. There is an incredible danger here, because if these folks don't catch on, then they will normalize their bad behavior.

The words ". . . without discerning the Lord's body . . ." can be seen in at least two ways. First, to partake in the Eucharist without a thought about Jesus and his death is not only to miss the point but also to risk debasing the meal itself. But there is a second way to think about these words that seem to echo loudly against the backdrop of the context: To share in the Lord's Supper without discerning the reality of the body—that is, the people within the Christian community comprising the body of Christ—is to come to a table that has been cut down to size by the people who prefer only the company of the ones who are like them. As a result, self-judgment emerges.

I've been in communion services where the table is approached with great fear. I've heard people say that if we don't approach the table with a pure heart and an appropriate grasp of a particular orthodox theology, then judgment will be rained down upon us. The table of Jesus, under those circumstances, can seem like the table of Zeus, where the slightest infraction can bring lightning bolts and scorpions.

Actually, Jesus does claim judgment for himself. Jesus once told some people that God had placed judgment squarely in his hands.

> The Father judges no one but has given all judgment to the Son, so that all may honor the Son just as they honor the Father. (John 5:22–23a)

When Jesus brings judgment, right is discerned from wrong, truth is discerned from falsehood, and righteousness is discerned from unrighteousness.

A woman is almost stoned to death for adultery. Jesus judges the duplicity of her accusers and she lives on, uncondemned. (John 8:1–11)

The story is told of a Pharisee who celebrates his own purity and contrasts himself to the sinful tax collector weeping in the corner. Jesus judges the Pharisee's hypocrisy and declares the righteousness of the sinner. (Luke 18:9–14)

A prostitute pours perfume—one of the tools of her trade—over Jesus, horrifying the respectable religious people who had invited Jesus to dinner in the first place. Jesus discerns her deep love and pronounces her forgiven of her sins. (Luke 7:36–50)

A thief hangs on the cross next to Jesus, sharing with him a slow and agonizing death. The man asks for neither forgiveness nor pity, but simply to be remembered. Jesus declares that before the day is out, they will be in paradise together. (Luke 23:42–43)

In these samples, judgment is rendered harshly and brutally by those who know nothing of Jesus' brand of judgment. Their judgment brings isolation, shame, and death, revealing their own hearts in the process. The judgment of Jesus cuts to the heart of the drama, pushing shame and condemnation out of the way and declaring what is true and right and beautiful. Human judgment can bring terror. The judgment of Jesus brings life.

Some might say that Jesus' own powers of discernment failed him when he chose the twelve. The disciples fumbled so much along the way that they ended up as almost comic figures at times in the gospels. Yet, Jesus chose them after his extended time of prayer. He included all twelve of them in what we call the Last Supper. If any group deserved a little kicking around before dipping the bread with Jesus it was those guys. But Jesus drew them, in all their sin and brokenness, and invited them to come and dine. Their deep followership would come later.

Judgment in the hands of humans is like a chainsaw in the hands of a two-year-old. That work is best left to those who know how to use the tools.

12

Same Height from the Floor

IN A CLASS THAT I occasionally teach I talk about making connections with the people in our natural environments. I describe the many neighborhood parties that are held in my driveway that give space for us to develop relationships with the people living near us. My goal with my students has been to open their eyes to the relational possibilities all around them as we think about the many ways that our churches might participate in the ongoing work of God in the world.

Just this week I ran into one of my former students who told me that he had taken my story seriously and, over the last six months or so, he and his wife had started their own neighborhood gatherings and had experienced some rewarding relational developments. Families who had lived across the street from each other for years met for the first time in my friend's driveway.

He told me of a family in his neighborhood who had immigrated to the U.S. from China four years earlier. They were delighted with these gatherings because they had believed, when they arrived in the U.S., that this kind of connection was normative in America. They imagined people from all walks of life and from a variety of ethnicities gathered together as neighbors and friends. They were deeply disappointed to find, upon their arrival, that Americans seemed to value isolation over community. These driveway dinners were a fulfillment of what their imaginations had envisioned.

What a disappointment it must be for someone to come to a church, following the longing of their hearts, only to learn that either they aren't qualified for the table of Jesus or that there is no table to be had.

Eating together has a leveling effect on people. Business meetings conducted over lunch are qualitatively different from meetings conducted in a boardroom. At a meal, everyone involved reveals their common need to eat and their shared vulnerability to the effects of starvation. Everyone has to eat and when we share a meal together we experience our co-humanity. I can't go back in time and stand on the level ground at the foot of the cross, but I can pull up a chair and sit next to others at the table of the one who died on that cross.

I am seeing the Eucharist as something much more than a penitential rite. I am seeing it as a profound invitation to the love of God that comes to us in the person of Jesus. The love of God brings rich and poor, healthy and sick, respected and discarded to a place of commonality in their shared humanity.

A few years ago a friend of mine invited me to attend a movie in one of those small Hollywood theaters that shows independent films. He brought another friend, a forty-year-old man who had just recently decided that the answer to his ongoing inner turmoil was that he was gay but had never accepted that reality. As we waited in the lobby for the movie to start, he took it upon himself to explain to me how his sexuality was something that was built into his life, how there had never been anything in his life that had caused this apparent preference and the way he was could never be altered. I suspected, since he knew that I was a pastor, that he was baiting me into a debate of some kind. He sounded like he was giving me a scripted presentation.[1]

I said, "You know, I don't really know how any of this stuff works. I'm not smart enough to figure out whether someone is born one way or another or if our sexual preferences come about at the flip of a coin. But that's not the place I want to start with you or anyone else. I can't begin in friendship with you for any other reason than that we are co-humans, made in the image of God. That's the only place I know to begin."

He just looked at me quizzically and didn't offer any more information. We attended the movie, went to lunch and shared great conversations. We left for home and got stuck in traffic, taking two hours to make the forty-five minute trip home. In that time on the freeway, he voluntarily opened his life up to me—a life of deep pain, abandonment and abuse. We had discovered a common ground as co-humans, and in that discovery there was the possibility for vulnerability and friendship.

1. It made me shudder just a bit when I thought of how our evangelistic efforts sometimes come across the same way.

There are a lot of well-meaning folks who seem to feel that in order to properly express love, everyone has to be accepted regardless of what is happening in their lives. I agree in principle, but not if love is the end of the conversation. Love is a beginning, not an end. When we respond to the love of God, we step out on a journey that will transform us rather than being accepted into a boundary-less affiliation that cares little about the state of our lives. That would be nothing more than tepid tolerance.

Tolerance has become a high value in our society. There is even talk here and there that lack of tolerance could become a criminal offense. Tolerance is a good thing, if it is firewall against hatred. It much better that you tolerate my religion, my ethnicity or my general weirdness than to shoot me for my trouble. For followers of Jesus, however, tolerance is an insufficient response to the diversity, brokenness, and sin of the world. Tolerance is not only a firewall against hatred and violence; it can also be a firewall against love.[2] I can tolerate you and put up with you and never love you. That is not enough for Jesus.

Perhaps a Eucharist grounded in love gives us a framework for our engagement with the world. When all are invited to the table of Jesus, no seat more privileged than the next, we sit next to one another sharing in common our humanity and the love of God that has been poured out to us. We don't come to the table alone but rather as a community of people fresh from the delusions and perplexities of the tower of Babel. We come having thought too much of ourselves and have ended up confused and in conflict with one another. Then we receive the invitation from Jesus, look into one another's eyes and wonder how in the world we could be drawn to this common table and loved so extravagantly and so recklessly that we find ourselves compelled to love one another.

~

At the time of this writing my home state, California, is in a financial disaster. Cuts are being made to social services, prison systems, and education. People are looking to the state to get it together and do the magic that will properly care for its citizens. I am wondering how the church might respond Eucharistically to this crisis.

Within days after Hurricane Katrina devastated the Gulf Coast of the U.S. in 2005, the government limped to the rescue. It was clear that the response to this disaster would be insufficient and the human suffer-

2. This idea came from a conversation I had with my friend, Dr. Craig Hovey.

ing would not soon be relieved. The press covered the government's weak rescue efforts and black eyes and bloody noses were handed out generously. But under the media's radar something else was happening: The church heard the summons of Jesus and joined his mission in the world.

Gulf Coast churches began networking together, racing joyously across denominational lines and began to tearfully care for the suffering community. Many church facilities had been damaged by the effects of the hurricane, yet those who were able swept out the water and started cooking soup, providing shelter, and delivering food, water, and clothing anywhere it was needed. One church on the edge of New Orleans, preparing to celebrate its first Sunday service in its new facility the week that the hurricane hit, dried up the water and invited the National Guard troops to bunk out in their empty sanctuary.

I was with a team that went to bring assistance during that disaster and watched as the local government workers struggled to repair downed power lines and clear roads and railroad tracks. But it was the people of the local churches who turned their fellowship halls into food warehouses and transformed their youth groups and Bible studies into special forces units, swooping into ravaged communities and giving a cup of cold water to people who just might have been Jesus in disguise.

The church's response was not mere compassion or a reflection of a social justice ideology. It was response that emerged from Eucharist. It was a response of love to co-humans, many of whom hadn't yet responded to Jesus.

I wonder what would happen in the Golden State if the churches said, "Look: How about if we take in some needy families and help them get back on their feet? What if we created space for certain prisoners who could be loved back into the land of the living? If schools can't afford to teach art and music, how about if the kids come to our place after school and learn some things about beauty and creativity?"

It occurs to me that many social services run by the government were originally innovations by the church. Caring for the poor and sick, visiting the prisoner, educating the ignorant were ministries of the church to the world. Various governments caught on to this and decided it was a good thing. Now we stand back and leave everyone to their own devices and wonder why it is all going to smash.

In his book *The Source of Life*, Jürgen Moltmann writes a moving introduction. He tells of being a German prisoner of war, held in Scottish and British camps until 1948. It was a time when all of his nationalism was crushed under the revelation of the Nazi regime's true agenda and his sense of guilt and shame was overwhelming. He reported how healing and forgiveness came into his life as the local villagers (all Christians, he claims) took him and his comrades in for the occasional home-cooked meal.

> In Kilmarnock the miners and their families took us in with a hospitality which shamed us profoundly. We heard no reproaches, we were accused of no guilt. We were accepted as people, even though we were just numbers and wore our prisoners' patches on our backs. We experienced forgiveness of guilt without any confession of guilt on our part, and that made it possible for us to live with the past of our people, and in the shadow of Auschwitz, without repressing anything, and without becoming callous.[3]

A broken, shamed young German officer comes to the table of humble Christians and finds himself unwittingly at the table of Jesus. Moltmann came to faith in Jesus during his imprisonment and went on to become one of the most influential theologians of the twentieth century. It was at those humble tables that Moltmann not only recovered his humanity, but found out an entirely new way to be human.

When I come to the table of Jesus I see others who are different from me yet share my broken, fearful humanity. Some are more damaged than others. At Jesus' table the gathered pilgrims don't have far to reach to put their arm around a brother or sister to participate in God's work of healing and wholeness. At the table we don't come to one another in our respective caste systems but rather as invitees whose shoulders touch at just about the same height from the floor.

I think the church's response to the world is Eucharistic. That's what makes it different from any other form of social justice. And maybe that's why we need to keep coming to the table.

3. Moltmann, *The Source of Life*, 5.

13

Beer Nuts and Holy Ground

COMMUNION WAFERS HAVE A shelf life of one year, according to some websites I have checked out. That's a pretty long time for something that is disguising itself as bread. The benefit in this appears to be that people can use what they want, stick the rest in a cupboard and retrieve them when they need them. It's actually a very advanced stage of convenience when you think about it.

Wisegeek.com says that in some parts of the world, communion wafers are sold in stores in the snack food section.[1] Just imagine: Body of Christ right next to pretzels, beer nuts and Twinkies. This makes sense to me, given the apparent ability of communion wafers to stay fresh for up to a year. A commercially produced cupcake from 1967 would probably still be edible today. Those things were made to last.

I wonder what is in those communion wafers? Various online manufacturers of communion wafers[2] claim that they are made only of water and wheat flour, and maybe some oil. I have a hard time believing that claim. Without some synthetic preservatives, that Bread of Heaven would start looking like the mold of Hades in a couple of days.

Regular bread, leavened or not, just doesn't last all that long after it's made. If bread sits out a while, you can make croutons out of it as long as green things haven't started growing on it yet. But after that, the bread is dead.

When it comes to Eucharist, I think the bread needs to be more like manna. As I recall, manna was the bread of heaven given to the ancient Hebrews after their rescue from Egypt. The people gathered it every day

1. http://www.wisegeek.com/what-are-communion-wafers-made-of.htm.

2. What does their factory looks like? Do they have a supervisor of consecration? Could making Body of Christ turn a devout worker into a cynic?

for food, but it wouldn't keep for even one day and no one considered inventing the refrigerator to solve the problem, which probably wouldn't have worked anyway because (A) I don't think God intended for manna to last longer than one day and (B) someone would have to invent an electrical grid which is another total complication.

The short shelf life of manna required the people to look for God's provision every day. They couldn't stock up on manna and then put their feet up and relax for a while. Every single day they would have to head out and gather the little flakes off the ground and eat them before they went bad. I suspect they got just a bit cranky about having to repeat this process every day, but one thing would be for sure: They'd have to remember that God was feeding them on a daily basis.

The bread at the Lord's Supper should be like that. We need to open our hands every day and receive the life of Jesus in fresh and new ways. Otherwise our forgetfulness will overwhelm us and we won't know who we are. We will forget how to see God in each day of our lives.

I figured out once how many days I had been alive. It's easy to do: Just take your age and multiply it by 365. You don't have to be exact—the sheer volume of days will cause you to pass out anyway. At this moment in time I have been alive for over 20,000 days. It's not only the number that stuns me, but also the fact that I don't remember most of those days. I can patch pieces of days together and come up with, what?—maybe seventeen complete twenty-four periods, none of which would make sense because it would be 1957 at breakfast, my wedding in 1972 at lunch, throwing up at school in third grade right around dinner, and sometime last week at bedtime. The days would just be a hash of events.

If you put your mind to it, you'd probably remember more crummy days than good days, because painful experiences really stick with us. This entire endeavor is really troubling, so maybe you'd better not do it after all. But the question keeps flying in my face: Where do 20,000 days go? They not only went by quickly, but they just disappeared. I find this disturbing on an existential level.

There's a fine Ignatian prayer called the Prayer of Examen. Ignatius of Loyola, a sixteenth-century Roman Catholic priest and founder of the order of Jesuits, instructed his monks to do this prayer on a daily basis, even if they had time for no other prayer. There are two components to this prayer: Consolation and Desolation. In Consolation, you consider all the life-giving experiences you've had in the last twenty-four hours. As you do that, you thank God for the gifts of life that he has given. In Desolation, you think of the things that have drained life from you (even if you've done those things yourself). You don't go to the place of thanking God for painful experiences (which would be either masochistic or just plain dumb), but rather asking why you felt pain in the first place. Was it because you lost something? If so, what? A sense of pride or self-protection? Friendship or opportunity?

In both aspects of the prayer, you also look for God's presence and work in that day. It's surprising when you do this, because you become more aware of God's life in yours. You get in the habit of remembering that God is real and doing things all the time, even if you aren't aware of what's going on. When I'm somewhat consistent with this prayer practice, my awareness of God being at work ramps up. I also write this prayer in a journal of some kind, because sure as shooting I'll forget the whole thing just like I forget what I had for breakfast some mornings.

For me, the Prayer of Examen is Eucharistic in that it requires me to hold out my hands to receive a fresh awareness of God. I can't store up the past like baseball cards in a cigar box. I've got to engage with the *now* of God. At the table of Jesus that awareness comes to life.

I teach a course on leadership for seminarians. Part of the course is about developing an awareness of what is going on all around us in the culture and in the people we see. I always do a short field trip to a local mall where we can observe the advertising and general hubbub of the place in order to see what promises are being made to people (look better, be happier and sexier if you buy this or that, etc.) and how the dynamic of the kingdom of God comes to bear on those promises. It's usually a pretty good exercise of awareness.

This week, however, when I took my class to the mall, it looked like a big flop. All the big banner ads that usually hang from every store were gone as the season was about to transition. All that the eye could see were simple signs announcing sales of 30–70 percent off, which is actually a pretty good deal if you are excited about shopping. I was sorry that the experience was rather sparse, but the students put a good face on it and made me feel like I hadn't let them down, which is my own brand of Desolation.

While we were debriefing the event at the mall entrance and planning to take off fifteen minutes earlier than usual, I noticed a young man standing at the fringe of our circle of twenty-five or so people. I didn't recognize him so I knew he wasn't one of my students. He was holding a leather folder and I wondered if he was mall security telling us we had to either buy something at 50 percent off or get out. But some other students began talking with him and I figured he was okay.

As we ended the debrief and just hung around for a while, my curiosity got the better of me and I went to see who this guy was. His name was Thomas and he was very friendly in an authentic way. He had heard us talking and initially thought we were a business group. Then he heard some references to God and wondered what in the world we were about. The students explained our mission and said that we were part of a theological seminary. He thought that was pretty great.

Thomas worked at the mall and was in this community alone and far from his family. He was only twenty years old and was making an attempt to carve out a life for himself. There was a real tenderness about him and he kept coming back to his appreciation for what we seemed to be about as followers of Jesus. We all talked a bit about faith and God, and then I asked him how we could remember to pray for him.

He appeared to ponder the question, and then I realized that he was fighting back tears. His eyes brimmed over and he wept. He told us about the suicide of his father a few years earlier and how it had devastated him, but his deepest concern was for his mother and sister. He grieved for them and struggled with the pain they were enduring while he was trying to make a life for himself on the opposite side of the country. The five or six of us who stood with Thomas found that our eyes were indeed opening up, but not in the way we had anticipated.

We helped Thomas see where God was present to him in his grief and struggle. We made an effort to dispel the notion that Thomas needed to jump through a series of hoops to meet God, but instead to only turn around and find that God was right there, arms wide open, welcoming his wandering son home. Thomas cried openly at that. Some students exchanged email addresses with him and made plans to come back to the mall for more conversation with him. No one attempted a sinner's prayer on the spot, but instead opted for relationship and the work of the Holy Spirit.

At the mall, another chair was pulled out at the table of Jesus. We had the privilege of pointing to a name card on the table that read, "Thomas." A place was already set and we were sent out to make that known to that lonely young man. That corner of the mall became for us holy ground. The experience went from observational to Eucharistic.

When God-in-the-burning-bush told Moses that he was on holy ground, Moses was already on there. God didn't instruct Moses to walk ten feet to his left, jump over a rock, do two handsprings and then he would find himself on holy ground. No, God told Moses what God had already done for him. The only thing left was for Moses to take off his sandals and feel the sacred earth beneath his feet.

Thomas was on holy ground that day. It was our privilege to help him see that. Right there in the mall, we all stood barefoot together, our eyes wide open to what God seemed to be doing.

14

Keeping the Porch Light On

IT IS PAINFUL WHEN someone we have loved and valued leaves us. It is one thing for a dear friend to move far away; it is another for that friend to say we are no longer friends. That is one of the deepest pains that Christian leaders experience when people move in and out so easily from their worshiping communities. The loss is often painful and rarely fully grieved. But we have to move on, regardless of the pain.

Painful separations happen in families as well, but there is a profound difference. When an angry teenager decides to do life on terms outside the family, the parents and remaining siblings yell, cry, justify, blame—and wait. The child doesn't just plug into another family up the street and take up being their kid for a while just because they have a better cable TV package. The child leaves, goes away, strikes out, and often ends up feeding pods to the pigs in a faraway land. Most families leave the porch light burning and keep an empty seat at the dinner table, hoping that one day there will be a familiar knock on the door.

Christian communities in the west are unique just because we often frame them consumeristically. We treat our communities like retail department stores, moving casually from one to the other based on inventory and sale prices. Numbing ourselves to constant departures is a way of coping with that movement and it is quite easy to airbrush people out of our family album. After a while, we forget that some people ever existed.

In churches, as in families, we often create *quid pro quo* expectations—something for something. In a family, we revisit our history of giving birth, potty training, wiping behinds, teaching bike-riding skills, paying for school and a whole host of other sacrificial offerings (because, as parents, we are *always* completely altruistic and never, never, never self-serving) and are devastated when our kids grow up and make choices we would never make. In churches, we welcome, baptize, counsel, befriend, visit, and teach, and then are devastated when the lure of the church up the street or the golf course at the edge of town draws those people from our midst or when they just lose interest altogether. How ungrateful everyone is!

When I was a pastor people would announce to me that they would no longer be a part of our church because of an unresolved conflict, disappointment in me as their pastor, a desire to get their kids into a better program at a church, or any number of other reasons. Often they would express a desire to stay in touch, remain friends, get together later, and generally stay connected just as though nothing had changed.

I would often explain to these people that their hope for maintaining those relationships was admirable but not probable. I didn't mean for them to think they had been excommunicated from any future connection, but rather that relationships in the community of Jesus are grounded in a common life of worship as opposed to common interest or general friendship. If your life is grounded in your common worship, it is challenging to remain connected when you announce that you no longer wish to share that life of worship.

There are many ways in which we leave one another. We move to another city, attend a new church, and sometimes we even decide to leave the faith. When we do that, we always leave behind those who decided to stay. Those who remain behind wrestle with emotions ranging from sorrow to a sense of betrayal.

Coming repeatedly together at the table of Jesus binds us in a way that transcends all other common points of connection. The image of the table as a place where all sit shoulder to shoulder, present because of invitation rather than qualification, eating and drinking the common life of Jesus, produces a shared life different from any other. Coming to that table over and over again creates an awareness of who we really are and allows us to become brothers and sisters.

Some, however, will come to that table and then not return—some for a while, others for good. What do we do with those we have loved and with whom we have eaten when they are drawn away by other voices and forces? Should we toss their name card in the trash, reset the place and give the seat to someone else? Having consumed body and blood once, are further meals no longer needed? Once someone walks away from the table, do we discard them from our common history?

> For it is impossible to restore again to repentance those who have once been enlightened, and have tasted the heavenly gift, and have shared in the Holy Spirit, and have tasted the goodness of the word of God and the powers of the age to come, and then have fallen away, since on their own they are crucifying again the Son of God and are holding him up to contempt. (Hebrews 6:4–6)

These hard words were written in the context of people whose comrades in the faith had left them to the devices of their persecutors. There were some who had shed their own blood because of their allegiance to Jesus and then there were some who called the whole thing a farce and walked away. I suppose it is impossible to restore someone to what they have tasted and shared when they have redefined it as something meaningless. Something else will have to happen for them to turn back again.

At some point in C. S. Lewis's *The Last Battle*, Susan informs her siblings that the whole Narnia experience was just a fanciful expression of youthful imaginations. She doesn't buy the story any longer and she disregards her own involvement in the great adventures she shared with her brothers and younger sister. As a result, the others move on without her. We don't know how her story plays out because we lose her before the books conclude. I liked Susan and grieved the loss of her presence.

I have a friend or two like that. We've shared some pretty deep stuff over the years in relation to our faith in Jesus, but now they've decided it's just not for them. They've moved on to other things—grown past it all, I guess—while I still ramble around in this big, roomy house of God. I don't know what to make of that and I can't figure out how they can come to the conclusion that the Jesus they claimed to know was merely an illusion.

But still I look for their place at the table. There is a faithfulness in Jesus that I struggle to find within myself. I think that Jesus, just like the father of the prodigal son, sets their place every night for dinner, flips on the porch light and looks off in the distance in the off chance that they'll be home soon.

15

The Riskiness of Grace

GRACIOUSNESS HAS ITS RISKS. Kindness and generosity often result in giving a person something that they cannot provide on their own. We cannot, however, control what the person will do with that gift.

So we raise our children, giving them life, time, money, wisdom, and values. Then they leave us to go smoke cigarettes and hang out with their hoodlum friends. We give money to a church or charity and then find out that someone ran off to Mexico with the cash box. I read somewhere that early Catholic missionaries risked their lives to preach the gospel to the Apaches, only to find out that the tribal leaders really liked the part of the story involving crucifixion, which they promptly used on their enemies.

A friend of mine was self-employed in the field of construction and found himself on a project near a barrio at the edge of our town. Every day he would stop in the little market in the barrio and buy something to eat. He was learning Spanish and he enjoyed talking with the locals.

One day he emerged from the market and saw a man sitting on a low wall, looking sad and dejected. My friend (a very generous person) walked over and talked with the man, and then told him that God had urged him to give the man ten dollars. The man was very grateful.

When my friend told me this story, I said, "He probably bought beer with the money."

Without missing a beat, my friend responded, "He probably needed a beer." My friend understood something about graciousness that I needed to learn.

The desire to control an outcome can override our desire to be gracious. It's very disturbing (yet somehow liberating) to discover how little we really control. Our kids have brains and motivations and we can't control what they think or, ultimately, what they do with their lives, regardless of how much we've done for them, how much money we've spent or how many stretch marks still commemorate the day of their birth. But we still produce children and do what we can to love and raise them up in a good way. We still give to the needy, to churches, and charities and don't have much of say in what they do with our gifts.

I wonder what was going through Jesus' mind when Judas reached over and dipped his bread in the cup that Jesus extended to him. He says to Judas, "Do quickly what you are going to do." Jesus gave Judas a place at the table and offered the bread and common cup, knowing full well that Judas was up to no good. Did Jesus know *exactly* what Judas was about to do, or was he just convinced that he had the freedom to take Jesus' graciousness out the door and stomp it into the ground?

I doubt that Judas was any different from the other disciples in the sense that he came at the invitation to follow Jesus and brought all his baggage with him. In the end, when he realized what a mess he had helped to create, he went to the religious leaders and tried to undo the deal. He gave back the money they had paid him, hoping to break the contract he had made with him. These were the guys who were supposed to help people with their religious life, which presumably included the processes of confession, forgiveness, and absolution. Instead, they offered this brilliant advice:

"What is that to us? See to it yourself."[1]

Left to his own, broken devices, Judas did see to it himself. In his grief and shame, he killed himself. Jesus' graciousness resulted in two deaths.

After all the panic, cowardice, betrayal, and death comes resurrection. Jesus does not rise to smite his enemies but rather to be reunited with his friends. He doesn't tell James and John, "There—how do you like that, you big dopes? Do you still want to be on my right and left?" He doesn't chew Peter out and ask him why he turned into a big chicken. Jesus seems to stand on both sides of graciousness. He gives generously and then stands with those who may have mishandled his gifts. That is a graciousness I'd like to learn.

What do I do when I leave the Eucharistic table? Do I really walk out the door to love and serve the Lord (as churches often remind us on Sundays just before lunch)? Maybe, on occasion. Mostly I leave to serve myself and keep hacking away at this life I am attempting to live. I suspect that Jesus

1. Matthew 27:4.

knows this about me. Maybe our priests and pastors should say to us as we take in bread and wine, "Do quickly what you are going to do."

When each of us finishes our meal and leaves the table of Jesus we go out to do what we are going to do. We take Jesus' graciousness and spend it in ways both good and bad. Regardless, when we return to the table, our place has been cleaned up and saved for us. The bread and wine is again offered to us by grace.

16

Primary and Secondary Signs

THERE IS A STORY in the Bible about the prophet Elisha experiencing the multiplication of food.[1] There are a hundred hungry people hanging around and a local man donates twenty barley loaves and some grain, clearly an insufficient amount of food for a crowd. Elisha has it distributed and everyone has plenty to eat.

This story is echoed in the gospel accounts, as Jesus multiplies loaves and fishes for a couple of mega-crowds, making Elisha's event look like a warm up to the real thing. People are amazed when it happens, especially Jesus' disciples. They are just starting to realize that something special is up with Jesus, although the other miracles and healings might have given them a few hints ahead of time.

Why do we need these stories? Maybe they suggest that God can do amazing things (although most of us already suspect that God, by definition, can do amazing things), but they don't prove anything. You'd have to have been there in order for anything to be proved. The stories just make us secretly ask if these could really have happened or if some overzealous early Christian just wanted it to happen badly enough that he talked someone into inserting the story.

I lean toward believing these stories because I keep meeting people who claim that such things have happened to them. I know of a couple of young women who decided to make peanut butter and jelly sandwiches and hand them out to homeless people in L.A.'s Skid Row. They prepared twenty-five sandwiches and somehow gave one each to fifty people, they claim. I was recently at a church in Phoenix where a group had just returned from an inner-city ministry trip and they reported that their almost-empty water jug kept producing cups of cold water even though

1. Found in 2 Kings chapter 4.

the water level was below the spigot. This kept happening until the water brigade showed up with more water. Then the jug dried up. That is the story they told.

I do understand why God would want to care for people—supplying food and water is an important way to do that. But I wonder if there isn't a deeper story going on when God seems to multiply the elements that sustain our life. This could be about primary and secondary signs.

My Greek Orthodox friend explained to me that primary and secondary signs are important to her family of faith. For example, making the sign of the cross is a primary sign; doing it with only your thumb, index and middle finger pressed together representing the Trinity is a secondary sign. The secondary sign is important in what it represents, but it isn't anything without the primary sign.

In the food multiplication stories, meeting the hunger needs of people might not be the primary sign. The actual feeding could be the secondary sign that is only significant when seen in light of the primary sign. The feeding is great, but eventually all those people went on to get hungry and thirsty again, so the miracle itself was of a temporary nature. I think that the feeding is secondary to a deeper story that is being written, expressed through Elisha and later repeated by Jesus.

John's gospel gives us some help with this:

> Jesus answered them, "Very truly, I tell you, you are looking for me, not because you saw signs, but because you ate your fill of the loaves. Do not work for the food that perishes, but for the food that endures for eternal life, which the Son of Man will give you. For it is on him that God the Father has set his seal." Then they said to him, "What must we do to perform the works of God?" Jesus answered them, "This is the work of God, that you believe in him whom he has sent." So they said to him, "What sign are you going to give us then, so that we may see it and believe you? What work are you performing? Our ancestors ate the manna in the wilderness; as it is written, 'He gave them bread from heaven to eat.'" Then Jesus said to them, "Very truly, I tell you, it was not Moses who gave you the bread from heaven, but it is my Father who gives you the true bread from heaven. For the bread of God is that which comes down from heaven and gives life to the world." They said to him, "Sir, give us this bread always."
>
> Jesus said to them, "I am the bread of life. Whoever comes to me will never be hungry, and whoever believes in me will never be thirsty. But I said to you that you have seen me and yet do not

> believe. Everything that the Father gives me will come to me, and anyone who comes to me I will never drive away . . ." (John 6:26–37)

Jesus' followers thought, at first, that food was the primary sign. Then they move toward believing that having the power to multiply food was the primary sign. But Jesus points them to something different. He points to a deeper work of God that mirrors the gift of manna that was given to their ancestors in the wilderness. The food itself was the secondary sign as was the multiplication of that food. The primary sign was Jesus, and the broad, expansive invitation that he gave to the world.

All who come to Jesus to receive him as bread will not be driven away, so he says. The people thought they were having the momentary satisfaction of having their stomachs filled. The reality was that they had been invited to the table of Jesus and it was the invitation of the ages. The places were set, the invitations sent out, and not a one would be chased off.

That which we see on the surface often belies a deeper reality, a greater story than is apparent.

It is easy to reduce what we see down to something we can contain and explain, either to embrace or to discard. It's simpler to do that than to seek to understand or to experience the reality behind and beyond our sight.

Body art has become so common that I barely even notice it anymore, except in moments of curiosity. On the surface, you have to wonder why people would waste so much money defacing themselves, when all those words and pictures will drift six or eight inches lower on their skin before too many years have passed. A beautiful woman's face inked on your shoulder when you are twenty-five looks more like the face of a wildebeest when it finds its way to your elbow at sixty-five. You have to think about these things.

My experience suggests that the tattoos we see so generally applied to the skin of people are not just whims of fancy; they tell stories.[2] Anyone I've asked will tell me the story of a particular tattoo or the series of stories that have resulted in an epidermal mosaic.

2. In a culture where faith in a larger story that gives meaning and purpose to all of life has all but died, inscribing your private story on your body may be the only way to believe that you really matter in the scheme of things.

Recently I was taken to a restaurant by one of my students, his wife and another couple. I was teaching an intensive course in Phoenix that met daily for a week, and the students were kind enough to see to my entertainment each evening. That night we landed at a restaurant that my friends had heard about but had yet to experience. It seemed like a nice place, and not many people were gathered on that weekday night.

Our waitress, young and attractive like all the other waitresses, came to take our order. On the inside of her wrist was tattooed the word "Blessed." A small crown adorned the top of the B, sitting at a slight angle. My friend asked her about it. I suggested there was probably a story behind the word, and she affirmed that there was. She was reluctant to take our time in the telling, but we encouraged her and she opened up.

She told us of a long-term relationship with a man that had turned violent and abusive. She was a virtual prisoner for a while, finally escaping back to her home and family. Legal action was underway and the pain of her experience was obvious. She felt "Blessed" because she now felt safe again. I secretly hoped that she would not seek out a replacement for this man and repeat the cycle, as is often the case. We thanked her for her story. My friend invited her to church.

I told this story in class the next morning, tying it into a lecture on pop culture and the church. My friend raised his hand to report that someone told him, that very morning, that the restaurant we visited had a unique practice on certain nights of the week. At some point, all the waitresses remove their clothing and continue their work wearing only thongs and other almost invisible dots of covering. The class members thought this was hilarious and took the opportunity to have a great deal of fun at my expense. I assured them that the night of nakedness did not take place on the prior evening. We were absolved based on ignorance. I called my wife at the break just to cover my bases.

While I'm grateful that everyone at the restaurant remained fully clothed during my visit, it was still an opportunity to hear the deep story behind what lied on the surface. That young woman could not be reduced to the sum of her tattoo and her skimpy dress (or lack thereof). The word "Blessed" inked into her skin was a sign of a deeper story that needed to be told.

~

In John chapter six, after Jesus feeds the 5,000, he says some more things about the food-multiplying event. His followers want in on this in a way that sounds like they want to be apprentices to a magician. They want to know how to do miraculous signs. Jesus challenges them on this point, telling them that they have focused on the surface event while missing the deeper reality. Yes, the feeding of the multitude was a sign—and signs point to something beyond themselves.

He claims that this particular sign points to him—"the bread of heaven." He says that he is the kind of bread that satisfies people forever, unlike the kind of bread they desire. His followers are puzzled and his critics get more critical over this.

There is another story related to this. It's an anti-multiplication story that appears early in the gospel accounts (Matthew chapter four). Jesus has retreated to an isolated place for prayer and fasting. During that time some temptations enter into his head, whispered by the voice of the devil, we're told. The temptation is to turn the stones on the ground into bread. That would not only satisfy Jesus' hunger, but would also open up the possibility of feeding the world.[3] Of course, doing that would derail Jesus' time of intimate prayer and communion with his heavenly Father. Jesus does not give in, but rather speaks out the deeper meaning behind the life-giving symbol of bread: "One does not live on bread alone, but on every word that proceeds from the mouth of God."

Bread. The body of Christ. Once again comes the struggle with Eucharist. The more I struggle the more deep meaning I find, and the more I catch glimpses of the deeper reality behind it all.

We experience the Eucharist together in a relatively small space, as most churches do. We come, not out of our qualification or self-induced purity, but rather at the invitation of Jesus to come and dine. Our table may be a small table, but it represents the real table that Jesus has prepared—a table that stretches though the ages and across all nations. It is a table with countless seats and place settings, because the invitation to

3. Henri Nouwen understands this temptation: "Oh, how often have I wished I could do that! . . . Aren't we priests and ministers called to help people, to feed the hungry, and to save those who are starving? Are we not called to do something that makes people realize that we do make a difference in their lives? Aren't we called to heal the sick, feed the hungry, and alleviate the suffering of the poor?" Henri Nouwen, In the *Name of Jesus*, pp. 17–18.

come is broad and sent to all people. It is a table where we receive the true bread of heaven, bread that will always satisfy.

John Calvin once suggested, in effect, that the miracle of Eucharist is not whether the bread and wine become body and blood or if Jesus is present in the elements; the real miracle is that any of us get invited to the table in the first place.[4]

When I think of the miracle of the feeding of the multitudes, I wonder if that isn't what is happening at a deeper level: The real miracle is not that there is more food, but rather that there are now more people at the table. Jesus often scandalized the religious elite by claiming that the down and out, the outcasts and sinners were loved and valued by God. The religious leaders didn't want those kinds of seats at their table because they thought it was only for people like themselves. Jesus says otherwise.

If the loaves and fishes are signs that point to Jesus, the bread of heaven, then maybe the receiving of that food is a sign of response to the invitation to Jesus' table. The multiplication itself appears to be a sign of the limitless nature of God's love and care and the sheer recklessness of his embrace. I don't recall any one in the crowd having to be interviewed before eating in order to determine their suitability. Everyone was fed.

4. Thanks to my friend Tom Parker for offering this summary. What Calvin actually wrote was: "Inquisitive men have wanted to define: How the body of Christ is present in the bread . . . A matter well worth all the words and the quarrels!—or so it is commonly thought. But those who do so think do not realize that the primary question in fact is: How does the body of Christ, as it was given for us, become ours? How does the blood, as it was shed for us, become ours? In other words, how do we possess the whole Christ crucified and become partakers of all his blessings?" John Calvin, *Opera selecta*, 1, 139, quoted in Parker, *John Calvin*, 64–65.

17

Enough Offense for Everyone

THE PART OF JOHN chapter six that really bothers me is that, after the miraculous multiplying of the food and then the freaky experience of seeing Jesus walk across water, many of the people turn and walk away. They see it all, they eat it all, and then they shake their heads and leave.

I'm not surprised that the larger gathering of people left. They ate the food, filled their stomachs and had their immediate needs met. Afterward, it was time to go home and get back to the business of daily life. I am disturbed, however, that Jesus' own followers would abandon him after all that had happened.

Jesus' words do get difficult, no doubt about it:

> Jesus answered them, "Do not complain among yourselves. No one can come to me unless drawn by the Father who sent me; and I will raise that person up on the last day. It is written in the prophets, 'And they shall all be taught by God.' Everyone who has heard and learned from the Father comes to me. Not that anyone has seen the Father except the one who is from God; he has seen the Father. Very truly, I tell you, whoever believes has eternal life. I am the bread of life. Your ancestors ate the manna in the wilderness, and they died. This is the bread that comes down from heaven, so that one may eat of it and not die. I am the living bread that came down from heaven. Whoever eats of this bread will live for ever; and the bread that I will give for the life of the world is my flesh." (John 6:43–51)

There is enough offense in this text to make everyone in the room upset. The people who come from Jesus' hometown are upset because they think he's being pretentious. How can he claim to be anything special when they saw him running around in his diapers when he was a kid? Others are offended because Jesus sounds like he's into cannibalism with all his talk about his flesh being bread. On one level, you can't blame the people for being put off by what Jesus has to say.

But why doesn't someone jump up and say, "Hold on, just a minute! We just experienced some pretty spectacular stuff, folks. Maybe there's more here than meets the eye. When was the last time you saw amazing things like this happen? Let's stick around with Jesus."

That does happen for the twelve disciples, but everyone else takes off. Maybe they were like addicts, losing their grip soon after the last fix. If signs were the end product for them, then they'd have to have signs all the time. Jesus' indication that there was something deeper going on was fine, but such language wouldn't draw a crowd or entertain the masses.

Taking the Bible seriously can be a real problem for people. People who believe that God is still working in the world in ways that challenge our rationalistic sensibilities can get very excited about seeing and participating in God's work. That's why we do things like pray for people to be healed from disease and injury. It's why we ask God to multiply our resources when there is physical need. I wonder, however, if we aren't just as vulnerable as those ancient followers of Jesus who got sign-happy and took off when Jesus didn't perform as they demanded. I'm not sure I'm any better than those folks. I think I'm just as much at risk as they are.

I suspect that's why we get this speech from Jesus in John chapter six. Without the deeper story, we risk stopping at the surface of what is really going on. It would be like searching for a friend's house and, when discovering the sign that indicated you were on the right street, you sat down at the base of the sign and figured you had gone as far as you needed to go. In the meantime, the real reason for your journey goes unnoticed and the party moves on without you.

I believe in signs and wonders—I do. I believe that God is still at work in the world and I'm humbled by his invitation to join in. But I tremble at the thought that I would abandon Jesus when he began to speak hard things to me and when I couldn't see the signs I demanded. I fear scrambling for more bread when the Bread of Heaven is standing right in front of me.

I hope that I will be able to answer along with Peter if Jesus ever asks me if I'm planning to turn and walk away to find a better deal somewhere else:

> Lord, to whom can we go? You have the words of eternal life. (John 6:68)

18

Getting My Order Right

THE LIVER IS THE filter of the body. To eat an animal's liver is, for me, the equivalent of snacking on the yellow end of a used cigarette. I will have none of it. What really puzzles me is that people would actually go to a restaurant and pay money for liver. I simply do not understand that.

My mother cooked liver and onions for our family at least once a month. My mom has always been a great cook, so I could never figure out why she would waste her skills on such an abominable meal. My father liked liver and onions, so that's probably why we ate it. My brother and I would have gladly taken beatings in exchange for going hungry on liver nights.

My brother is eight years younger than I am. From his earliest years he has been a steak and potato man. When steak was cooking in the kitchen (my mom could make the best pan-fried steak in the world), Dave was all smiles. So his face was filled with delight the day he came in to see and smell what he thought was steak cooking on the stove.

He was probably eight at the time, which would have made me sixteen. I was talking with my mother as she stood at the stove stirring the onions that smothered and evidently disguised the liver that my poor brother had mistaken for steak. Apparently the abundant smell of onions in the pan diverted his attention from the grim reality beneath. When he cheered loudly that we were having steak for dinner, my mother just looked at me and smiled, saying nothing. It occurred to me that while I was enjoying the subterfuge, my mom just might be evil.

As our family gathered around the dinner table, Dave was practically singing as we finished our nightly prayer for our food. Dad, Mom, and I were all in on the secret, and poor Dave was heading for his doom blindly and with great joy. We waited as he prepared for his first bite. I was having so much fun that I forgot that I would soon be eating liver as well.

With an expression of sublime expectation, Dave shoved the first bite of liver into his mouth. Immediately all the blood left his face, his eyes rolled into the back of his head and his gag reflex kicked in. On top of that, we all laughed at him. Dave cried, not because of our laughter, but because of his deep disappointment that there would be no steak. Not only would there be no steak, but there would be liver. Please, let the beatings begin.

To my parents' credit, they let Dave off the hook that night. I don't know what he had for dinner, but it wasn't liver. I think they feared he would go into convulsions. I wondered why he and I hadn't thought of this ploy years earlier rather than suffer the revolting taste of bovine internal organs. As I recall, we quit having liver after that. God bless Dave.

It's a real shock to get something served to you that you didn't order. At restaurants, I send the wrong order back to the chef, even if I did just take a bite out of it to make sure it was the wrong meal. When I get home with a bag of hamburgers for the family, there's always one that has or doesn't have cheese, depending on the orderee's preference.

I have ordered more things from Jesus than you can imagine. I've ordered happiness, health, money, job placements, friends, and the unyielding obedience of my children, but the order never turns out as I requested. I've received happiness, but pain was all mixed up in it. I've been offered jobs, but they weren't the ones I asked for, yet they somehow turned out better than what I imagined. I've had money once in a while, but with it came a shallowing of my dependence upon God. Jesus just can't seem to get my orders right.

I have, however, occasionally prayed what we call The Lord's Prayer, and there is a clause in there about God's will being done. Maybe I've repeated that back to God enough times that he thinks I really mean it. I used to think that God's will was like a hidden, mysterious document containing a secret code, and if I could just dig it up I'd have everything figured out. But I've come to believe that God's will has more to do with what God desires and intends rather than with what he has decreed and hidden. God hasn't set us up so that we'll stumble all over ourselves trying to find his secret will and generally failing at the attempt. And what God wants is always a lot better than what I want.

Just the other day I was thinking about my own career experiences. There have been times when I've gotten what I've wanted by strategic planning, political posturing, and sheer personal desire. The qualitative results of those career accomplishments have ranged from just okay to totally disastrous. However, there have some times when things have been served up to me and, while I didn't see them coming my way, God's fingerprints seemed to be all over them. Those things have always turned out to be the best things in my life. They were not, however, the things I would have ordered up for myself.

I cringe at how arrogant I've been at times, pulling up a chair at Jesus' table, leaning back and dictating my meal request to him. I wonder how often I've stormed off, dissatisfied and hungry because I didn't eat the meal he brought to me, thinking it to be substandard or unworthy of someone like me.

> Whoever, therefore, eats the bread or drinks the cup of the Lord in an unworthy manner will be answerable for the body and blood of the Lord. (I Corinthians 11:27)

Lord Jesus, Son of God, have mercy on me.

19

Resolving Dreams

My dad told me of a recurring dream he had as a young man. He was sitting in one of the rear seats of a San Francisco street car—the old kind, with steering mechanisms on each end. He realized that the car was moving faster and faster, shaking from side to side, and there was no conductor to be seen. In fact, my dad was the only person on the street car.

He fought his way to the front end in order to take hold of the brake and stop the car from crashing. As soon as he reached the front, he discovered that the car was moving the opposite direction at the same breakneck speed. He kept moving from front to back in a panic, only to find the car reversing direction every time he thought he was about to take control. Then he would wake up.

Dad said he began to look forward to this dream to see if there was a resolution. There never was, and the dream eventually disappeared.

I've had those kinds of recurring dreams which people sometimes say are about a subconscious attempt to work through conflicts and insecurity. I have one dream that continues to visit me: I have abruptly returned to my business career after an absence of many years. I arrive at my office wearing a suit and carrying a briefcase. As I enter, people I used to know greet me and act as if I've never been gone. I go to my desk, review phone messages and mail, and realize that I have absolutely no idea what is going on. I am an emperor with no clothes and I'm pretty sure I'm about to be discovered.

There was one dream I had for a few years that was charming, mysterious, and haunting. In the dream the entire neighborhood next to my house had disappeared and there in its place was an old, three-story, prairie Victorian house standing alone in a large empty field. It was painted blue with white trim and, though it might have been an eye-catcher in its day, it was now in need of some repair. Each morning I would look out my window and wonder about that house and if there were any inhabitants. I wasn't frightened, but rather deeply curious.

One day I wandered over to the house and knocked on the door. An elderly woman answered, dressed as though it was 1895. Her face was kind and welcoming and she invited me inside. The house was charming, with ornate wood interior and patterned area rugs, but obviously neglected for many years and barely maintained. When I told the woman of my curiosity, she welcomed me to explore the house to my heart's content.

Upstairs I found that one of the entire floors was opened up as one room. In it were many pieces of beautiful antique furniture, lined up in uneven rows as if they were in a warehouse. The pieces were dusty but exquisite in their design and vintage. I lingered over each piece, checking out the structure of the dresser drawers and the artistic bevel of the mirrors. The sun shone through the grimy windows, creating a mysterious, filtered light. In my dream, I was in that room for hours.

I worked my way back downstairs and found a doorway leading to the basement. During my exploration I discovered that one corner of the basement was built into a natural rock formation that had a small, cave-like tunnel that led to the outside yard. I suddenly realized that I had been in this house before when I was a child. I recalled that I used to play in this basement and crawl back and forth through that tunnel. It was a moment of remembrance that impacted me deeply, but I didn't know why.

This dream recurred quite often and I always enjoyed it. There were some modifications to the dream, but the themes remained, for the most part, in tact.

I shared this dream with a woman I knew who was supposed to be pretty good at sorting out the meanings behind dreams. After hearing the details, she suggested that the symbols in the dream were particularly significant for a Christian because of what they represented. A house, she said, is often representative of what is in a person's inner self—the heart. She added that an elderly woman is symbolic of the church. She thought that these images revealed that the church was imbedded deeply in my heart. She went on to say that the antique furniture symbolized the forgotten treasures in the life of the church and the experience in the basement suggested that the church and the call of God had been in my life since I was a child.

The woman then said that it was quite possible that the dream would stop when I stepped out into that which God was leading me.

I gave consideration to her words and then, since Thomas is my patron saint and I only believe in things I can verify with my own dark, cynical mind, I tucked it all away in the back of my brain.

Within a year, I planted a church and left my business career. The dream stopped and has never returned.

As I continue to play with the image of my life of faith being framed by the eternally stretched out table of Jesus, I imagine Jesus welcoming me to the same seat, over and over, yet whispering words in my ear that require me to consider that he would like to move me to another seat. Out of resistance to change, fear of the unknown or just plain old habitual behavior, I keep returning to the same seat. Then, one day, his words get to me and I take the risk of following him to a different place at the table. It's the same table and the new seat isn't better or worse than the old one, but it is different. There are different people around me and new conversations to be had. The food and drink are still rich and nutritious, but now served in different plates and cups. I wonder why Jesus has moved me here—maybe to be taught, perhaps to welcome a newcomer or even to share something of my life with my new acquaintances. I don't know the purpose of any of this until I pull out the chair and sit down.

There is even the possibility that there is no purpose to the move except that Jesus wants me to be there. That has to be enough.

> ". . . In this life and in the world to come, those who follow Jesus will receive everything they want, if what they want is to follow Jesus."[1]

1. Neuhaus, *Death on a Friday Afternoon*, 58.

20

When Jesus Leaves the Table

OCCASIONALLY I LOOK UP from my meal and notice that Jesus is gone from the head of the table. I wonder where he is, but it's really none of my business. I'm sure he can take care of himself.

Other times I think I see Jesus but soon realize that an imposter has entered the scene. The person looks a bit like Jesus, has some of his mannerisms but there's something amiss and it takes a while to put my finger on it.

Having come to the table, we sometimes get distracted by the silverware and china and quit casting our eyes to the one who has invited us to the table. We stop looking at him, hanging on his every word, and look at one another, influencing, arguing, debating fine points of self-constructed theologies and even complaining about the quality of the food and the service of the restaurant. Then we look up again, and Jesus is gone.

Jesus has been gone before. Once he shared that final meal with his friends, he left them: First arrested, then interrogated, then beaten, and finally crucified and buried. All this he did without them. The meal was still in their stomachs but Jesus had left the table. Even after his resurrection return he would leave again, promising the presence of Holy Spirit. But his physical presence would disappear from view.

What is very disturbing to me is that imposters keep showing up to take Jesus' place at the table. He's not out of our sight for two minutes before some wannabe Jesus pops out and starts talking trash about God. Most disturbing of all is to look around and see some of the people at the table actually listening and considering the new words being spoken. Sometimes, I am one of those people.

The replacement Jesus can be slick, like "Buddy Jesus" in the movie *Dogma*. He's smiling, winking, and giving a thumbs up because, by golly, everything's going to be okay. Other times it's the secret code Jesus, slyly informing us that we can have health, riches and a great life if we just find the secret of belief and fill up our faith bucket to the right level. Then there is the I'm-disappointed-in-you Jesus, who looks around sadly, grieving that we humans have once again let him down and aren't living up to our potential. It's just so hard to really love people like us.

So we listen and buy in. Not always, but often enough to be dangerous and enough for us to lose sight of Jesus altogether.

Paul the Apostle ran into this and had to yell at the Christians in Galatia for swapping Jesus out for a shoddy replacement.

> You crazy Galatians! Did someone put a hex on you? Have you taken leave of your senses? Something crazy has happened, for it's obvious that you no longer have the crucified Jesus in clear focus in your lives. (Galatians 3:1, *The Message*)

Jesus' good friend John ran into the same problem when some folks he had invested in were giving some thought to the idea that Jesus was really just an illusion sent from God and didn't really suffer and die like a run-of-the-mill human. John had to remind them that he was an eyewitness to all the events of Jesus, and he was pretty sure that his eyes hadn't deceived him.

> We declare to you what was from the beginning, what we have heard, what we have seen with our eyes, what we have looked at and touched with our hands, concerning the word of life— this life was revealed, and we have seen it and testify to it, and declare to you the eternal life that was with the Father and was revealed to us— we declare to you what we have seen and heard so that you also may have fellowship with us; and truly our fellowship is with the Father and with his Son Jesus Christ. (I John 3:1–3)

Apparently replacing Jesus with an imposter is not a new story.

I wonder what it is about the real Jesus that we don't like? I think we like the healing part, especially if it happens to us. We probably like it when Jesus kicks around the religious elite, especially when we think we're not one of them. We like the salvation and eternal life part of Jesus, but there are some things that come along in the bargain that aren't so attractive, like suffering and death.

Jesus' friends struggled with this right up to the point of Jesus' arrest. At one point they seemed to think that they had finally figured out Jesus, but he wasn't so sure.

> Jesus answered them, "Do you now believe? The hour is coming, indeed it has come, when you will be scattered, each one to his home, and you will leave me alone. Yet I am not alone because the Father is with me. I have said this to you, so that in me you may have peace. In the world you face persecution. But take courage; I have conquered the world!" (John 16:31–33)

Yes, Jesus has conquered the world, but there is still persecution, there is still suffering and death. We like the Jesus who has conquered the world (especially that part of the world that keeps us from health and prosperity) but we're a little sketchy on the Jesus who reminds us of the inevitability of pain. It seems to come with the territory.

I am increasingly nervous about Jesus' absence from his table. If I can't see him because he's way down at the other end, welcoming more strangers and stragglers to dinner, that's great. But if I can't see him because I have turned away and left Jesus to a new crucifixion while welcoming in his cheap, tricked-out replacement, then I shudder.

I know people who reject Christian faith because they have rejected the caricatures of Jesus that have come their way. They were taught as children to believe something that now seems bizarre, so they turn away. They were hurt by some people wearing Jesus disguises, so they run from all things that hint at faith. They listened to popular critiques and constructed their own straw dog Jesus and then shot it to pieces with a bazooka. And so we keep crucifying Jesus.

And we wonder why we miss his presence at dinner.

21

"What Did That Man Do?"

AT THE SEMINARY WHERE I work there is a bronze sculpture of Jesus in front of the library. The artwork is on ground level because Jesus is being laid back on the cross before he is actually crucified. There are two men on either side of him, one fixing Jesus' arm to the place where it can be nailed to the rough wooden cross beam, the other bringing the hammer down to impale Jesus' other arm. The face of Jesus is distressed and even a little fearful. All this was laid out on the ground for people to view and touch in life-sized proportions.

One day while on campus I observed a young family—father, mother, and little boy about four years old—standing around the sculpture and quietly talking among themselves. The parents were interested but distracted by their own adult conversations. The little boy, however, was apparently intrigued by the drama portrayed in the art because he stood silently for a while, staring at it. As I passed by, I heard him say to his father, "Daddy, what did that man do?"

I didn't stay around for the father's response because it was one of those intimate, parental teaching moments. I must confess, however, that I didn't want to hear what the father would say. It might have been profound, insightful, and life-changing for his son, or it might have been a cliché that brought confusion and distress. The young father looked pretty sharp to me, so I'm betting on the first option.

Nevertheless, I've thought about that brief encounter many times. For we who have been western Christians for many years, the image of Jesus being nailed to the cross is standard theological fare, while for a four-year-old boy, it is the stuff of horror movies. We glibly pass by such representations while children see it all for what it is: A gruesome act of violence and terror. The sight of Godzilla eating all of New York is nothing compared to a man being held down and nailed to a cross.

What would you have said to that little boy? There are several possible answers to the question, "What did that man do?" and also several possible four-year-old responses:

1. He died for our sins. *He what? What's a sin? What do you mean* our *sins?*
2. God sent Jesus to die because he was angry about the sins of the world. *Why would God do that? Why didn't God just put all the bad people on a time out or spank them? Would God do that to me?*
3. God had to have the death of a good person like Jesus because God is just. *Who says that God has to have something? His mom? What does* just *mean? When God is just do good people have to die?*
4. Jesus had to die so that God wouldn't wipe out everyone because of their sins. *I think God is mean and has a bad attitude.*

I've heard variations on these answers and you probably have as well. I often wonder how we reconcile the God who demands crucifixion with the Jesus who invites us to his table.

I am aware that theories of the atonement abound and I've wrestled with a number of them. It's a touchy and puzzling subject and folks often get riled up over the differences in perspective. People often camp on one theory regarding why Jesus died as though such a tragic, complicated set of events could be laid out in a neat formula that make our questions and struggles unnecessary. While there may be a number of theological interpretations about the death of Jesus, it seems to me that there is one obvious reason why Jesus died.

Jesus died because he was born.

Jesus' followers surely expected that he would die one day, if only from old age. They thought he was the Messiah, but that didn't mean they thought he was one with God.[1] For them, the Messiah was a special person, but still just a person. Death was as much of a guarantee for first-century Messiahs as it is for twenty-first century librarians or stockbrokers or pool

1. N. T. Wright points out that the Hebrew term *Messiah* or its *Greek* version, Christ, did not carry with it a necessary connection with divinity: "The earliest Christians, those who had followed Jesus during his short public career, had never imagined that a Messiah would be *divine*." He goes on to state that there was, however, ". . . an astonishing shift, for which again nothing in Jewish traditions of the time had prepared Jesus's followers . . . They said that he was the unique embodiment of the one God of Israel." Wright, *Simply Christian*, 116–17.

cleaners. All human beings, on the occasion of their births, are handed a ticket to their own funerals.

No matter what a person believes about Jesus—a good man, a prophet, the reincarnation of Krishna or the incarnate Son of God—it was a sure bet that his birth in the manger guaranteed his death at some point in the future. The fact that his death came at the hands of the religious leaders and the government makes sense: Jesus threatened their power centers by declaring that there is no God but the God of Abraham, Isaac, and Jacob, and that the kingdom of this God trumps the kingdom of Rome and the control towers of Jerusalem. That's dangerous talk and people get killed for such things.

I lean toward the incarnate Son of God belief. I really do believe that Jesus is somehow one with God in a way that I cannot comprehend. I believe that God has made himself known to the world in the person of Jesus. As Paul the Apostle wrote,

> He is the image of the invisible God, the firstborn of all creation; for in him all things in heaven and on earth were created, things visible and invisible, whether thrones or dominions or rulers or powers—all things have been created through him and for him. He himself is before all things, and in him all things hold together. He is the head of the body, the church; he is the beginning, the firstborn from the dead, so that he might come to have first place in everything. For in him all the fullness of God was pleased to dwell, and through him God was pleased to reconcile to himself all things, whether on earth or in heaven, by making peace through the blood of his cross. (Colossians 1:15–20)

If we believe that Jesus was, so to speak, God-in-the-flesh, then it means something very important that God started this project out by being born as a human person. When human persons are born they are destined to die someday. That means that God wasn't just rolling the dice with Jesus. When God becomes human, his death is an inevitability.[2] And

2. Ray Anderson describes this incarnational death: "The Father sent the Son into the world to assume [human] death, to experience that death, to die that death, in order that the death of humans might become the death that God dies. God, who has no death to die because God is the source of life itself, assumed human death as the consequence of sin in order to die that death." He also points out the inevitability of Jesus' death, since he shared our common humanity: "Jesus, thus, had his own death to die. He did not simply die the death of others vicariously. He died the death that was part of his humanity assumed at conception and birth." Anderson, *The Soul of Ministry*, 90.

when this God on the cross willingly goes to his death and lets the tyrants of the world have their way with him, their power seems to be the winner until Jesus is raised from death. That pretty much sticks it right up the noses of the ones who think that it all begins and ends with them.

I don't know what I would have said to that little boy. I hope that God gave that young father a big dose of wisdom right on the spot because he really needed it. He was also going to need a few cups of coffee, because his son was likely to have trouble sleeping that night.

Jesus invites his friends to his table in an intimate setting. Then he marches out and is brutally killed, dashing all their hopes right into the ground. Did his followers have any kids who asked them questions like, "What did Jesus do, daddy? Why are they killing him?" At the time, would their answers be any better than mine? How do you make sense of such a death, especially when you are buried in terror and grief? It would take a while for something theological to emerge from an event so tragic.

At the end of the gospel of John, the disciples are out fishing after the death and resurrection of Jesus. It's a weird scene in my mind, yet perfectly understandable. After the roller coaster ride they'd been on, maybe they just needed a little taste of normal. Fishing was normal for them and perhaps they even forgot for a little while about all that had just happened.

But then Jesus shows up, and once again he invites them to his table, this time on the beach for a fish barbecue. It takes them a minute or two to recognize him, but the invitation to the meal should have been the big tip off. In the midst of the disciples' attempts to make sense of all that had happened, Jesus simply invites them to breakfast. And once again, they eat.

Without further explanation or interpretation, Jesus cleans up the dishes and tells Peter, "Feed my lambs." That is enough for now.

22

Getting Sin on Us

WHY WOULD THERE BE a table that Jesus has prepared and a church that has honored that table for 2,000 years, and still people walk on by, ignoring their invitation and gorging themselves on junk food instead? Is this table meant only for me and people like me? Are we smart while they are stupid? Does God like us better than other people? Are we better than those who pass by? I have a hard time believing that, especially about myself. Just ask my mother. She'll set the record straight.

When I was born my mother gazed lovingly at me and asked my father, "Do you think he'll do all those awful things that boys do?"

My father replied, "You'll never know, dear."

Well, Dad, that's true, unless your grandmother lives across the street from you, which mine did. So when I was four years old (the year of my Lutheran baptism), my grandmother gleefully called my mother on the phone to announce that she was watching me relieve myself on the hubcap of a car that was parked in front of our house. My mother was mortified (mortifying my mother seemed to be a life pattern for me), less by my barbaric actions than by my grandmother catching me before Mom did.

I can't imagine God looking at this scene and saying, "Now, there's a young man who's going places. I'll make sure he gets a seat at the table." It seems like there would have been many other qualified four-year-olds in line in front of me who never peed on their neighbors' cars.

There seems to be a long-standing debate among Christians about who is in and who is out. We speak of being people who are chosen by God. There is a lot of that kind of talk in the Bible, but we keep asking what we are chosen for. Is it that we Christians have been chosen to go to heaven when we die while everyone else has been born to become fuel for the fires of Hell? Seems like an odd arrangement.

After the delight of the creation account in Genesis chapters one and two, everything hits the gutter in chapter three. Then, all the way through chapter eleven, it's one failed attempt after another as people try to put the train back on the track. Adam and Eve have kids, maybe hoping that the next generation will get it right. Instead, murder is invented. God washes away all the evil people of the world and gives Noah and his family the shot at a major do-over. No sooner are they back on dry land than they reintroduce broken relationships, cursing and alienation. Then the people of the earth, discovering how incredibly brilliant they are, take matters into their own hands and build a tower so that the whole world can celebrate their advanced technological skills. That doesn't turn out too well for them either.

Then, in chapter twelve of Genesis, something amazing and yet understated takes place. God taps a wandering Aramean on the shoulder—Abram was his name—and tells him that he has a new destiny for him.

> Now the Lord said to Abram, "Go from your country and your kindred and your father's house to the land that I will show you. I will make of you a great nation, and I will bless you, and make your name great, so that you will be a blessing. I will bless those who bless you, and the one who curses you I will curse; and in you all the families of the earth shall be blessed." (Genesis 12:1–3)

It seems like God is saying, "Look. You folks can work from now until the end of time and you'll never get it right. Leave it to me. That's the only hope."

So, while there might be both blessing and cursing on the horizon, God has all the families of the world in mind when he elects Abram to be the father of a new nation through which blessing will come. There is clearly a choosing, but it's a choosing that has the entire world in mind.

Lesslie Newbigin helps me with this.

> The Bible, then, is covered with God's purpose of blessing for all the nations. It is concerned with the completion of God's purpose in the creation of the world and of man within the world. It is not—to put it crudely—concerned with offering a way of escape for the redeemed soul out of history, but with the action of God to bring history to its true end. The Old Testament therefore is full of visions of a restored humanity living in peace and happiness within a renewed creation. These visions are not of an otherworldly bliss, but of earthly happiness and prosperity (Pss. 82 and 144), of wise

> and just government, of a renewed nature in which kindness has replaced the laws of the jungle (Isa. 1:1–9).
>
> But this universal purpose of blessing is not to be effected by means of a universal revelation to all humanity. There is . . . a process of selection: a few are chosen to be the bearers of the purpose; they are chosen, not for themselves, but the sake of all.[1]

Abram (later to be called Abraham) and his descendents (later to be called Israel) are chosen, not just to have a club of their own with restricted membership, but rather to bring blessing and benefit to the rest of the world. We Christians see ourselves as being adopted into this family of God, so this kind of choosing must apply to us as well. Perhaps being a Christian isn't about who gets in and who doesn't. In fact, the question of in and out is probably none of our business anyway. Our business is about taking God's choice seriously and turning to bring his blessing to all the families of the world.

Of course, this could just be feeding into my discomfort with the idea of excluding people. Or, it could be that the place I've been offered at the table of Jesus isn't just about me. It's also about me letting all those passers-by know that there is a place set for them right next to me. Even if they've committed murder or adultery or robbed the local Winn-Dixie or peed on their neighbor's car, there is a seat at the table reserved for them right next to mine. They don't come to the table to re-energize themselves for more murder or adulteries or robberies or random peeings. They come to be changed. They come to find out who they really are—beloved sons and daughters of God.

I recognize that this is all counter-intuitive. It would be like accepting an invitation to a dinner party and looking forward to good food and close, intimate conversation. When you arrive, you are served a delightful meal and the conversation is rich and inspired. Then your host says, "Now that you've finished your dessert, let's run out into the streets and invite anyone we see, because I've got a ton of food left in the kitchen."

Before you know it, a couple of neighbors who had been home watching *Gunsmoke* reruns are now at the table, still in their pajamas. Right next to you is a homeless woman someone pulled out of a dumpster and she smells like twelve years' worth of used sweatsocks. And, of course,

1. Newbigin, *The Open Secret*, 33–34.

there's the guy who was working on his car and never went to college and thinks he knows everything. Now we're all at the table together.

This is a difficult arrangement because we thought this was about us. On top of that, we had experienced a unique chemistry that is now completely destroyed by the addition of these second-tier invitees. We will never have what we were experiencing earlier. We have something different with these new people and things will never be the same for us.

Maybe the lesson for us is that we can have the most loving, inspiring churches and services and the most intimate, connected small group fellowships and enjoy them to the fullest as long as we're willing to let them die. Once we realize that we've been chosen for the sake of the world that God loves, all our preferences for safety, coziness, predictability, and sameness get machine-gunned on a regular basis. Getting everyone cleaned up and synthesized chemically doesn't seem to work when Jesus is on the job.

I've talked to some folks who find the idea of people coming to church or to the Lord's Supper or whatever without cleaning themselves up first, to be offensive. I've talked to pastors who won't counsel couples who want to get married but are living together, giving the argument that to do so would be to get their sin all over us, thereby making God mad.

This kind of thing puzzles me, since we follow Jesus, who got our sin all over him.

23

Priests for Everyone

MARTIN LUTHER, SO I'M told, loved good food and good German beer.[1] In the movie *Luther*, a slender Joseph Fiennes plays Martin, which is strange, since Martin Luther was supposedly quite the tubby boy.

I don't know if beer-drinking significantly influenced Luther's theological journey, but I suspect that the joy he found in food and drink might have caused him to reflect on the expansiveness of God's grace.[2] He was also a bit irritated about his own family of faith, the Roman Catholic Church, and had an ongoing name-calling battle with the Pope. Even though Luther was a priest, he became very critical of the priesthood and thought it should be dramatically revised.

Luther believed that a priest was needed to administer the sacraments, but not really for anything else.[3] He capitalized on these words from the New Testament book of First Peter to make a case for a new kind of priesthood:

> But you are a chosen race, a royal priesthood, a holy nation, God's own people, in order that you may proclaim the mighty acts of him who called you out of darkness into his marvelous light. (I Peter 2:9)

These are an amazing bundle of images: A family of people, chosen; ministers both kingly and priestly; set apart as a community large enough

1. As a Lutheran baptizee, I tip my hat to Martin.

2. I also recall that Luther was a depressive type, which might also explain his attraction to beer and food.

3. Luther wrote, "Some can be selected from the congregation who are officeholders and servants and are appointed to preach in the congregation and to administer the sacraments. But we are all priests before God if we are Christians. For since we have been laid on the Stone who is the Chief Priest before God, we also have everything He has." Luther, "Sermons on the First Epistle of St. Peter," 62.

to be called a nation; a people with a new identity as God's own. All this, not for their own sake, but in order to proclaim all that God has done, and to make that proclamation to anyone who will listen.

Why would a priest also carry the title of royalty? In the life of ancient Israel, kings and priests were a separate class of people. It seems, however, that when you are part of the family of the king, royalty must be assumed. It is God who is king, and as his people, we are part of the royal family. But what about the priesthood?

The ancient priests of Israel were one of the twelve tribes, the tribe of Levi. Unlike the other tribes, the Levites didn't share in the inheritance of the land that God had given to Israel. They would be supported through the gifts that the people brought, but the true inheritance of the Levites was the Lord (see Deuteronomy 10).

This text in First Peter implies that all who follow Jesus are chosen, but not for their own sake; they are part of God's royal family, but in many ways give up what others might feel entitled to; they are set apart as a body of people, and that set-apartness is for God's larger purposes in the world. This is very different from seeing the church as a religious club that has an exclusive membership.

Martin Luther loved this idea of the people of God as a priesthood, and referred to it as The Priesthood of the Believers. For him, with the exclusion of administering the sacraments, everyone was a priest in the family of God. This did not sit well with the Roman Catholic Church of the day, since they had an entirely different way of looking at the priesthood.

Generally, Protestant churches would say that they have no priesthood and that all their members are ministers, which is mostly untrue. We still set up church governments that look like a version of the priesthood and expect our pastors and leaders to do things that mere mortals are unable (or unwilling) to do. There is not much difference between Christian leader as professional priest and Christian leader as professional CEO. You can call a turnip a hamburger if you want, but you won't fool me. You know I'm right about this.

At the same time, the idea of all followers of Jesus taking this royal priesthood thing seriously is compelling. Again, the image of the table of Jesus helps me with this. Each one responding to the invitation of Jesus sits down to become a member of the royal family. As such, they are commissioned to proclaim to the world that there are place settings abounding for them. We come to realize that all the real estate, 401(k) accounts, lottery winnings and buried treasure pale in comparison with the inheritance that is the Lord. Once again, it is all counter-intuitive.

Of course, if we really believed these kinds of things, a lot of Christians would end up in jail because we wouldn't go to war any more (it's hard to shoot bullets at people whose place setting is right next to yours) and would probably ruin the national economy by stopping our greedy, consumeristic spending compulsions, especially at Christmas, when the retailers and the Fed all hope that we'll bail out the Gross Domestic Product (happy birthday, Jesus). But I digress.

I think that Luther was on to something. Maybe we don't need a priest if we think of a priest as a human mediator between people and God. But isn't there a priestly service that we bring to one another and to the world? Luther thought it was acceptable for a person to earn a living as a butcher, then serve for a while as a priest, then go back to chopping up ribeye steaks. If we don't serve one another in a priestly way, then maybe we are abandoning ourselves to the ravages of individualism and consumerism.[4]

I recently took part in a retreat with a group of seminary students. At the end, we prepared to share the Lord's Supper together. We gathered in a large circle, each of us seated in a chair. In the center of the circle was a table with the communion elements spread out. My friend Tom, who was leading the retreat, spoke engagingly of the Lord's Supper and gave us a framework for thinking about the meal we would share. Then he took the bread and wine, walked to one of the students, knelt before her and, saying her name, served her the body and blood of Jesus. She then took the elements and walked across the circle to another student, serving that student in the same way. This went on until all were served.

This was a different experience than what I had experienced in both Catholic and Protestant churches. Instead of one priest, all became priests and for that moment in time, looked another person in the eye and proclaimed the mighty acts of him who called us out of darkness and into his marvelous light. And although all were involved, it didn't lapse into the individualistic, self-service mode that too many Protestants have embraced. It was sacred ground for me, and another moment when the Eucharist came alive.

4. I borrowed this from Dallas Willard, in a brief conversation with him a few years ago at a conference. I asked him if he thought the idea of church membership was dead. He said (right off the top of his head, as really smart people often do), "If we do not provide people with a way to belong, then we leave them to the ravages of consumerism."

24

No Heretics Allowed

HERETICS ARE CLEARLY NOT allowed at the table of Jesus, or so people sometimes say. It seems to go something like this:

"Well, hello. Welcome to the table of Jesus."

"Why, thank you. It's good to be here."

"Isn't it great, coming all together with a common mind and heart?"

"Um, what do you mean?"

"You know, all on the same page with our beliefs and doctrines."

"Oh, right. I suppose that is a good thing."

"Yes, it is. So—aren't you glad that we can all agree that Jesus was 5′ 4″ tall?"

"Really? I've always thought of him as taller than that. More like Nicholas Cage than Danny DeVito."

"Hmm. Yes, quite funny. So you don't believe that Jesus was 5′ 4″ tall?"

"No, not really. I think he was taller. Definitely taller. Would you mind passing the barbecue sauce?"

"Hold on. Excuse me everyone! Can I have your attention! This guy thinks that Jesus was taller than 5′ 4″."

[sounds of chairs flinging backward; a woman screams; a young child throws up in his Spaghetti-Os]

"What shall we do, friends?"

"Kill him! Burn him! Boil him!"

This might sound a bit ridiculous, but we Christians have been tough on people who haven't, by varying standards, been thinking rightly. For example, in 1553 John Calvin had his former friend Michael Servetus arrested because old Mike didn't buy into the doctrine of the Trinity. To help him get his thinking straight, the council that judged him had him burned alive.[1] In our day people have been judged to be heretics for thinking out loud about God's involvement with the world and with Jesus' presence in and among unworthy human beings. Of course, we no longer burn our heretics at the stake. We just ruin their careers.

Jesus, of course, was judged to be a heretic. He was called a blasphemer, accused of being in league with Satan, a low-life who associated with other low-lifes, and a general troublemaker. The accusers colluded and saw to it that Jesus was executed for his heresies. We look at that drama and believe that the many were off base and corrupted while the one man Jesus was in the right.

Ever since, we've reveled in our confidence that we, the many, are always right when standing against the one. I wonder if there is anything for us to learn from our own history? More importantly, is the way we organize information in our heads our qualification for coming to the table of Jesus?

I once took a small group of my students to lunch during a course I was teaching. As we were eating and talking, some of them began dismissing a large religious group for their heretical doctrines. I was more interested in my excellent burrito than the conversation, but I eventually chimed in by asking them why they considered these folks to be outside of God's favor. I was told that it was because of what they believed. Since I have a dark heart and am inherently evil, I pressed on.

"So is having right belief what secures our salvation?" They affirmed that it was.

"Is accurate and consistent information about Christian faith what makes us right with God?" They knew I was up no good, and since their grades were currently in my hands they hesitated, but eventually agreed that accurate information was very important. I continued weaving my sinister web.

"There are something like 2,500 Christian denominations in the United States alone, each one claiming to have some grip on doctrinal correctness that makes them distinctive from everyone else. I'm just wondering which Christianity is the right one?" I returned to devoting myself to my lunch, feigning disinterest in the topic.

This caused no end of controversy, but since they were fine people they didn't haul me out to the streets, my burrito unfinished and undi-

1. To his credit, Calvin asked that Servetus be executed by beheading, a more merciful death. His request was denied.

gested, tie me to a light pole and set me ablaze. But we did have a good conversation about the way we sometimes concretize our doctrinal positions and crash everyone else against them so that we can be sure we're right when others must be wrong.

I'm not saying that our ways of expressing our belief don't matter. I think they do. However, our violence against those who see things differently troubles me. If a person thinks that God hates all unmarried, sexually active people and wants to kill them, then I probably won't lock arms with that person and visit people in the hospital who are dying of AIDS and minister to them in the name of Jesus. If a person believes that God would just as soon obliterate sinful human beings because of sin but is restricted from that because of the goodness of Jesus, then that person translates God as a monster. Our belief systems do matter for something.

When Jesus talked with the woman he met at Jacob's well in Samaria[2] and then spent a few days with others from her town, he sat at the table with people whose belief system was different from his. They worshipped in different ways from purely Jewish people and Jesus was fully aware of that and pointed out the difference to them. Then he introduced himself as the Messiah they had been waiting for and gave them some of his time. I don't recall any stonings or burnings in that story.

Paul the apostle says,

> . . . in Christ God was reconciling the world to himself, not counting their trespasses against them . . . (II Corinthians 5:19)

These ones with many trespasses are being reconciled by God to himself and he doesn't count their trespasses against them. We, however, seem to spend a lot of time and effort counting trespasses and smacking one another in the head with them. For a people drawn into the peace, the *shalom*, of God, we are still drawn to violence.

I'd like for us to come to the table of Jesus rather than the table of interrogation and accusation. I'd like to see us thank Jesus for his gracious invitation and marvel that we've been invited to this great banquet. Then, we can debate all we want about the things of doctrine and cognitive belief, argue and learn from one another, then continue coming back to the table to keep the conversation alive. The only smoke we should smell should come off the marshmallows that we roast for dessert.

2. Read this story in John chapter four.

25

Ordination

TWICE THIS MONTH I have brought the homily to the morning mass at the ecumenical Catholic church that has befriended me. This morning was my second Sunday to serve there. I arrived, as usual, at 7:45, fifteen minutes before the first mass. There is always a legitimate priest there who presides over the service. I sort of follow him around, deliver my homily on cue, and then assist him in the rest of the mass. Father Peter was on vacation, so another priest would normally come to lead the service. Today, however, was different.

At approximately thirty seconds to eight, my friend Tony (the deacon) came up to me and said, "You'll have to preside over the mass today. Our priest forgot to show up."

I replied, "Can I do that?" I could feel bubbles forming in my blood vessels.

"Sure," he said. "We had a Lutheran and an Episcopalian preside once. I guess that means you can do it."

Since I am an ordained pastor, that somehow made me qualified to lead the service, including leading people in the Eucharist. Since I normally just tag along with the priest, I really didn't know specifically what to do. Tony ran and grabbed the notebook that gives the step-by-step instructions. Even priests need to be prompted, it seems.

He walked me quickly through the process, and I nodded my head idiotically as though I knew what he was saying. The bottom line was that they were stuck if I didn't do this. I really had no choice. Since there weren't that many people in the morning mass, I figured I could outrun them if I goofed things up too badly. To cover all the bases, Tony did a pre-announcement letting everyone know that I would be leading the service. The people are very nice, so they all thought it would be just fine.

After the processional, some prayers, and in the middle of the reading of Scripture, I was sitting on the dais when the priest who was supposed to preside walked into the back of the sanctuary. I figured that he would now join us and I'd be off the hook. Instead, he disappeared into the back, re-emerged and walked out the door, leaving me to my own devices. I considered that I might find him later and slug him on the arm for deserting me.

This church celebrates a high liturgy and is very respectful of all the things that take place during the mass. But underneath it all is an informality that feels safe, symbolized in the formal vestments worn by the clergy and the shorts, jeans and t-shirts worn by the people. Laughter and joy is never far from the surface and that's a good thing, since I needed a little laughter today.

Things really went quite well. Tony let me wear his new alb and the stole he chose for me was in various shades of green that looked very environmentally friendly. I thought I looked rather dashing, in a religious sort of way. I didn't make very many mistakes, the servers helped me along, the people laughed at the right times during my homily, and the Eucharist was served without spillage or blasphemy. That was a big relief.

While I love this church, it isn't technically the church I regularly attend. Yet the people receive me as one of their own when I arrive, calling me Pastor Mike, Father Mike, or just plain old Mike. It all works for me. They also tease me about being a closet Catholic and tell me that they wish I'd join up with them permanently. It makes me feel quite good, actually.

During the reading of the Scripture and just before serving the Eucharist, the strangest words popped into my mind: *I'm being ordained today*. It was funny that I would think that, because I am already ordained. Unlike other ordinations, however, mine was pretty odd. I had just planted my church and was trying to embrace my new identity as a pastor. I really wanted to feel comfortable in my new skin and it wasn't coming easily. So I told the head of my tribe of faith that I wanted a formal ordination. They don't put a lot of stock on those kinds of ceremonies because they believe that God does the ordaining and the ceremony is quite unnecessary. But for me, it had become necessary.

I met the head guy at his office, and three other leaders took a couple of minutes to come join us. We had two major issues to resolve: (1) Where to find the glossy certificate in the storage room; and (2) Locating a pen that would actually write on the glossy surface. With minutes we had solved these ecclesiastical dilemmas and I was summarily ordained. Off I marched with my certificate.

So, this morning, I heard those words in my head and wondered what in the world they could mean, if anything at all. I served the Eucharist, holding up bread and wine, body and blood, and proclaiming the Lord's death until he comes. The people were served, we made the sign of the cross, we rejoiced in God's goodness and then moved toward the close of the mass, which is always preceded by some announcements.

There were several announcements about a youth group car wash, a fund-raiser event and a couple of other things. Someone yelled out their thanks that I led the mass, and everyone clapped and cheered. Then a woman in the back said, in a voice loud enough for everyone to hear:

"Pastor Mike, today was your ordination."

The people clapped again and I almost passed out. I told them what had passed through my mind and still didn't know what to make of it all. We ended the mass and prepared for the next ritual: Walking two blocks to Starbucks for coffee with my friend Tony and Father Arturo, who was supposed to preside at the mass. I asked him why he didn't jump in to save me.

"I had five different services to lead today, and I forgot about the early mass," he said. "So, when I walked in and saw you up front, I just figured that you had it covered." I was flattered at his confidence.

I still don't know what to think about what happened. It seems weirdly coincidental that I would be in the midst of writing this book and then have this Eucharistic ordination experience with my Catholic friends. My wife says it's probably an important puzzle piece and I should watch for the other pieces yet to come as the picture gets clearer.

I don't think I'm a Protestant anymore. I can't think of what I would be protesting.

26

Manners at the Table

WE WERE FAIRLY INFORMAL at the dinner table when I was a kid, yet there were basic manners that were expected when we gathered to eat. My grandmother, however, was of the ancient school that believed a certain level of decorum was mandatory and certain violations were punishable by death or worse.

My grandparents were not rich people. My grandfather had been a poor preacher and then a struggling businessman his entire life. When he died, they were living in a nice, tidy but small mobile home in southern California. While my grandmother had to learn to make do with very little, she saw to it that the little she had was clean, set out properly, and not taken lightly. Maybe the family would have to eat porridge for dinner, but at least the bowls would sit on a lace tablecloth.

My grandmother and her sisters, my aunts, could cook a glorious dinner out of tree branches and moon beams if pressed to the task. On holidays they would join together in someone's kitchen, gabbing and arguing, flour and baking soda floating through the air, aromas unspeakably rich and savory finding their ways to sniffing noses and hungry bellies. They were the food wizards of a bygone era and I love the memory of those kitchen extravaganzas, although I was always kicked out when caught on one of my early raiding attempts.

When Grandma made a pie, all of time stopped, the moon and stars gaped in wonder and the earth went silent. I should have gone silent, on that summer afternoon in 1962, when I said too much and received too little for my trouble.

My numerous and rambunctious cousins were up from San Diego, and we played in Grandma's front yard while she prepared her amazing cherry pie, my eternal favorite. When it was time to dish out the portions, I catapulted myself inside the house, leaving my unworthy cousins in my wake. As Grandma dished out the pieces, I recklessly and foolishly uttered words that I have wished for years that I could take back:

"I want the BIGGEST piece."

Grandma, who I knew loved me dearly, would not put up for a moment with any such selfish demands. There was not a weak bone in her body and her principles were shored up with rebar and steel beams. She did not waver nor did I consider for a moment the possibility of a tantrum or efforts at renegotiation when she replied,

"Then you get the SMALLEST piece."

And so I did. I wanted to cut my throat and then slaughter my cousins (especially the girl cousins) who would surely mock me when they discovered the insidious consequences of my crime. Violating manners anywhere near the table was, for Grandma, an offense not to go unpunished.

Are there manners at the table of Jesus? I suspect that Jesus is fine with a little sloppiness and an occasional belch. I wonder, however, how he feels about our bad mouths when we pull up our chairs and hold out our hands for more? What is his response when we trash talk people down the row or speak against those who are absent altogether? Do our portions change? Do we even notice?

I have this image in my mind of we who return often to the table of Jesus pulling up our chairs, smiling sweetly, and asking for things to be passed our way. Our conversation is normally civil, but suddenly things become different. It is election season, and new permissions seem to be given to the ones calling themselves followers of Jesus. We might be citizens of the kingdom of God, but we're also Americans, and as Americans we embrace our right to hate and bear false witness as long as it is during an election year and our venom is reserved for the candidates and party we do not prefer.

This is actually more than an image for me, because election years come around often enough for this to be a recurring theme. With the invention of the Internet, I receive scores of messages from my Christian brothers and sisters who tell me why I must fear and hate the candidate they don't like, a candidate who is very likely the Anti-Christ and/or Satan (depending on what bent eschatology you want to embrace) or just plain evil and stupid. With transmittable videos, I can now receive obviously doctored films of candidates seeming to say things that they aren't really saying, providing apparent evidence of their dark, evil hearts.

In the last election, I received so many of these kinds of things that I finally snapped, wrote a response to the propaganda I had received, and hit REPLY TO ALL. I never heard back from even one of the forty million recipients, but at least the emails quit coming for a while.

It isn't that I object to their preference for a particular candidate. I object to speaking, writing and forwarding things that foster hatred, slander and the bearing of false witness. While I support the debates about important issues, I am hurt when I see and hear remarks (and video clips) that show how we Christians don't mind playing by the rules of negative ad-speak when it suits us.

I wonder why, during these election years, I never receive any messages encouraging us to pray for our future leaders. Never got one. Not a one.

I seem to recall that Israel got in some pretty deep trouble by playing politics by the rules of the world. Everyone else in the neighborhood had a king, so the Israelites wanted a king. Other nations had big armies, so Israel built an army. The surrounding culture had more interesting and sexually active gods, so Israel co-opted a few just for good measure. In the end, they lost at that game because that wasn't what they were made for. They were made to be God's people and, as such, to bring blessing to all the families of the earth through their worship, devotion, and unique way of living under the shadow of Yahweh's wings.

What are we Christians made for? Is it to hate, slander and bear false witness in the name of Jesus? Election year or not, I sure hope we're made for something better than that. In fact, I'm pretty confident that we are.

I know that this kind of bad behavior comes at other times also, but election years are like Mardi Gras: Normally sane and sober people take advantage of the opportunity to run around like drunken, crazy people (actually, many of them *are* drunk and crazy) and then pretend to return to business as usual the next day. I just wonder why we Christians don't question our own behavior during these times. It is interesting that in the United States, our presidential election season ends just prior to Advent. We should think about the irony of that. Welcoming Jesus into the world right after we spew election year sewage should bother us just a bit.

Could the worst manners at the table of Jesus be despising someone that Jesus loves rather than putting our elbows on the table?

27

Eucharist and Prayer

Most of us have had the experience of meeting friends at a restaurant or coffee shop. Maybe three people plan to meet, but only two arrive on time. They begin to talk, creating a mini-community right there over their decaf grande mochas, and a unique chemistry emerges. They are enjoying each other's company and connecting in a deep and important way. Then friend number three shows up. They are delighted to see their friend and make space for the new arrival. The conversation begins anew, but it's all different now. The two have become three and the interaction changes. For these friends, it becomes better, richer, more diverse, and interesting. What the two alone had is now over and gone, never to be retrieved. But what is new is better.

Prayer has been as difficult for me as Eucharist. I've had good times of prayer, but I can remember most of them which means they haven't happened as often as they should. I've journaled my prayers, read the Psalms as prayers, squinted my eyes, and made wrinkly faces to be effective at prayer and it still remains difficult. My wife prays like she is breathing; it just seems to come naturally for her. My prayers are like breathing under water.[1]

When I pray I often think of God waiting stoically while I come up with the right words to express whatever it is I have to say to God. Then I shut up and listen, just in case he wants to respond. Of course, if he does, I will probably miss it because I'm already thinking about something else. My attention span in prayer is pathetic. Doing prayer with just God and me is intimidating. Maybe that's why I dodge him so frequently.

1. "For the unbelieving husband is made holy through his wife . . ." (I Corinthians 7:14). I'm banking on this one.

I think I'm mostly wrong about the individualistic nature of prayer. I'm learning that our western way of thinking has drawn us into a mindset that elevates and values the power of the individual (and the individual's rights) over everything else and may have created a distorted view of our life in the economy of the kingdom of God. I'm learning about this in relation to the Eucharist and I'm learning about this in relation to prayer.

When I pray individualistically, I have to imagine God being disconnected from everyone else, or at least working in such a way that it feels like that to me. But aren't there a lot of other people already praying by the time I show up? I believe that to be so, and therefore, prayer is a pretty gigantic conversation that is already in motion.

Jesus said,

> When you are praying, do not heap up empty phrases as the Gentiles do; for they think that they will be heard because of their many words. Do not be like them, for your Father knows what you need before you ask him." (Matthew 6:7–8)

I accept the idea of God's omniscience. God's knowledge is limitless, so I can accept that he already knows what's going on in my head before I start praying. So if God already knows, why do I have to pray? He might be just sitting there mumbling, "Yes, yes, yes. Tell me something I *don't* know."

What if, along with his unlimited knowledge, my Heavenly Father also knows what I need because the other folks in the conversation have already told him? What if my prayer for myself is preceded by the prayers of others? What if my prayer for others draws those hurting ones into God's presence through prayer? What if prayer is not individualistic but communal?

I am imagining myself going to the place of prayer and realizing that I am jumping into a conversation that has already begun. Everyone sitting around the table, including God, turns and looks as I approach. They grab an extra chair and I join the gathering. It's all different now, of course, but God seems to think that it's different in a better way. The relational chemistry has been modified but that is his intention. Then I speak my concern to him.

"God, I hate to mess up the discussion, but I have this really important thing going on in my life."

"Yes," says God, "I know all about it."

"Oh, right," I say. "I forgot—you know everything."

"Well," he says, "that's true, but Fred and Mildred were just telling me about your situation."

"They were?" I look over at Fred and Mildred and they smile at me. Mildred pats me on the hand.

"Yup, they were." God takes a sip of his venti caramel macchiato. "I was already at work at your problem before you got here. But it's great to see you and hear your voice."

"Wow." I would take a drink of coffee to hide the fact that I don't know what to say, but I forgot to order anything. "So, um, how are you going to fix it?"

God's eyes get big. "Fix it? Who said I was going to fix it? I said I was working on it. If you want it fixed then you don't need me—you need a troubleshooting manual."

"So you're not going to fix my problem?" I'm thinking I might need something a little stronger than coffee.

"I didn't say that either," says God. "Look—if you want me involved in your life, then trust me. The outcome probably won't be what you expected, but in the end you'll like it better. Trust your friends who keep talking about you behind your back and then you keep coming into the conversation."

I understand that the difference between prayer and my little story is that when we pray we don't typically have multiple channels we can use so we can talk with each other as well as with God.[2] But there is something important, I believe, about us considering the power of our communal, shared faith. We might even have to challenge our Jesus-and-me way of thinking when it comes to finding forgiveness and salvation.

~

> One day, while he was teaching, Pharisees and teachers of the law were sitting nearby (they had come from every village of Galilee and Judea and from Jerusalem); and the power of the Lord was with him to heal. Just then some men came, carrying a paralyzed man on a bed. They were trying to bring him in and lay him before Jesus; but finding no way to bring him in because of the crowd, they went up on the roof and let him down with his bed through the tiles into the middle of the crowd in front of Jesus. When he saw their faith, he said, "Friend, your sins are forgiven you." (Luke 5:17–20)

2. Like various social media and Internet applications allow us to do when we're supposed to be paying attention to our professors or the person who is leading our invigorating two-hour meeting.

All we know about the man is that he was paralyzed. He never says a word so we can assume that everything about him was paralyzed, including his mouth. His friends are carrying him around on a gurney and they drop him through the roof so that Jesus will heal him. Jesus does heal him, but he also pronounces that his sins are forgiven. And on what basis? Not that the man prayed a prayer seeking forgiveness, but rather that the friends expressed trust in Jesus. In fact, they don't say anything to Jesus either. He just translates the look on their faces and reads *faith*.

Apparently no one told Jesus that you are not supposed to do this kind of thing because we are individuals and as such, we are responsible for ourselves. But Jesus violates that way of thinking by forgiving and healing a man based on the faith of the man's friends.

Prayer just might be like that. There is a great cloud of witnesses out there, and prayers to God abound. I suspect that many of the good things of my life have come about because of the faith of my friends. Maybe Jesus has seen my prayer for someone else as an act of vicarious faith. If so, then Jesus isn't hamstrung by my weaknesses and inabilities. I have friends who are always lowering me through the roof to the feet of Jesus.

But I'm still invited to this table, this table of Jesus, this table of prayer, where conversations abound and faith emerges. It is a conversation that changes when I show up and, although I'm always late to the party, Jesus seems to act like things got better upon my arrival.

Like the Eucharistic table, the table of prayer is expansive. Maybe they aren't different tables after all.

28

Coming Late to Dinner

There seem to be those who appear to come to the table of Jesus and never return. We don't really know what is happening for them. There are others who leave but return much later. Theirs are the stories in which we are privileged to share.

My grandfather left the table of Jesus for a very long time. He had sprouted from several generations of Christians—some who were pastors and leaders—and he responded to what he believed was God's call to a vocation of pastoral ministry. My mother, the oldest of his three children, was raised in a pastor's home.

Along the way Grandpa got hurt, as many pastors do. He moved in and out of his role as a pastor, staying long enough to dedicate me when I was an infant. It broke my mother's heart when the family took a hiatus from church life in her late teens. Church had framed her world and she grieved the loss of that life and community. Grandpa finally gave it all up sometime after I was born. He tried his hand at some business ventures over the years, but none of them amounted to anything.

He and my grandma occasionally attended church, but Grandpa's heart wasn't in it anymore. When my family started attending church with regularity in my early teens, it was the same denomination in which Grandpa had gotten hurt so many years earlier. He often made fun of our church, which infuriated my parents, who were trying to make a go of religious life for themselves and were finding it appealing.

It was many years after his death, when I had experienced pastoral life for myself, that I began to understand his pain. He thought he was doing what God had called him to do and then it all seemed to crumble. Grandpa was probably his own worst enemy and had caused some of his own problems, but—don't we all? It still hurt him, I'm sure.

Grandpa was an important presence in my life. He and my grandmother always lived in close proximity to us so I saw them often. Yet, he and I never really spent time together or shared any adventures. Except one.

When I was sixteen I was put on restriction for the zillionth time, probably for coming home late from a date, which I did often, although the girl who lured me toward my curfew violation is now my wife, so it turned out fine in the long run. It was the night of my high school's homecoming game and I, as a consequence of my crime, was sentenced to attending a wedding for someone I didn't know with my family. I was ecstatic. I negotiated every angle I could think of, but my mother, borrowing from my grandmother's red-hot core of immutability, gave me her stony-jawed look which sealed my fate with no hope of pardon.

But Grandpa was no happier being at that wedding than I was. I wondered if he had also been put on restriction for some grandfatherly crime. He was a significant and influential presence in our extended family circle, especially in the eyes of my mother. At the reception following the wedding, he and I were standing against a wall, both looking miserable.

"So, Mike," he said, "what would you be doing tonight if you weren't here?"

I sighed grievously to underscore my pain. "I would be at the homecoming game. We're playing our chief rivals, and I'm missing it to be here."

Grandpa thought about this for a bit, then asked, "Is the game almost over?"

I looked at my watch. "No," I said. "It's just about the end of the first half."

He thought about this again. He looked around the room until he located my mother, then walked over to her and said something. In short order he returned to me.

"Let's go," he said. "We're going to the game."

I looked over at my mother who shot me an indecipherable look. It didn't matter. The patriarch had spoken. We were going to the game.

When we arrived at the stadium at my high school, the home side was packed out, so we sat on the side of the opposing team. Grandpa bought the tickets. There we were in our long sleeves and ties, sitting on the wrong side of the stadium, and I couldn't have been happier. We won the game, the people around us said cruel and vindictive things, but I didn't care. Grandpa and I went to the game.

My mom is no pushover. I argued my way through most of my childhood and rarely won a case, and when I did, I suffered for my victory. So when Grandpa swiftly changed the course of my history, I knew I was in the presence of raw power. Anyone who could stop my mother in her tracks was kin to Superman. And when he dropped me off at home, I didn't get any lectures from anyone. After all, I was with the King.

I've often thought about how a man with such influence impacts a family when his heart is broken and he can't bring himself to return to Jesus' table. My mom met my dad, freshly discharged from the army, when she was nineteen and married him six months later (I suspect she was anxious to move away from the pain she shared at home. No matter her motivations, her decision to marry my dad worked out pretty well for me[1]). Her younger brother became an alcoholic atheist, but a whiz at business. The youngest brother was only five years old when my folks got married, so his experience was completely different. In his adult years he became, and still is, an enthusiastic Christian. My grandmother had to adjust from being a pastor's wife to being the wife of a man who couldn't seem to find his place in life.

When Grandpa turned seventy, something happened to him. One day he got up off the couch, jumped in his car, and drove down to our little church and had a conference with our pastor. No one knew about this conversation but the two of them. On the following Sunday, Grandpa did something that rocked our entire family.

He insisted that he and Grandma attend our church that morning. That seemed strange to her, but she went along with it. When they arrived, my parents were surprised but pleased to see them. As the service began, they entered the sanctuary and sat together. There were the requisite hymns, special music, and offering, with a sprinkling of announcements. Then the pastor, before starting his sermon, informed the congregation that there was someone present who had something to say. Grandpa rose to his feet and approached the pulpit.

No one knew what to expect. I was not in attendance that morning, since my wife and I lived over a hundred miles away at the time. But I have often imagined him moving into that pulpit and placing his hands

1. I am the first-born child and was born, by the way, five years later, just in case you were wondering.

on the sides, letting something almost lost yet familiar work its way back into his skin, as though the wood of the pulpit had been waiting to inject its authority into him. He looked out at the expectant crowd and began to speak.

He told them of his wanderings and his pain. He confessed his anger at God and his disdain for the church. He asked forgiveness for his mockery and expressed his regret at hurting the people he loved. He explained that he wanted to come back to the family of faith he had so long ago deserted. Then he waited. The old-fashioned, conservative people of that small, insignificant church did the only thing they knew to do.

They killed the fatted calf. They wept and embraced my grandpa. They showered him with love and rejoiced that one who had died now lived. They pulled out his reserved seat at the table, dusted off the crumbs and set him down. They passed the plates with joy and gladness, thanking Jesus for his faithfulness.

Grandpa seemed to make up for lost time. He started a prayer ministry at the church and taught a Bible study for a while. He became a prominent fixture at that church and was loved by the fine people of that faith community.

Two years later, he died.

I'm a lot like him, my grandpa. That worries my mother a bit, but it doesn't worry me. I come from good stock.

29

The Shadow Meal

In all three synoptic gospels (Matthew, Mark, and Luke), Jesus winds up his last meal with his friends by saying,

> "I tell you, I will never again drink of this fruit of the vine until that day when I drink it new with you in my Father's kingdom." (Matthew 26:29)

Bible scholars have differing views about the meaning of Jesus' words here. Some suggest he is referring to the meal they will share when the kingdom of God comes in its fullness and all will be gathered at the great banquet feast of the ages. Others say that he is speaking of his post-resurrection reunion that will come quite soon. I lean toward this latter interpretation.

Luke lets his readers know that Jesus fully re-engaged with people after his resurrection. At one of his early appearances, Jesus reveals that he is still kin to all of them by expressing his need for food:

> While in their joy they were disbelieving and still wondering, he said to them, "Have you anything here to eat?" They gave him a piece of broiled fish, and he took it and ate in their presence. (Luke 24:41–43)

In the first chapter of Acts, Luke opens his sequel with the account of Jesus spending forty days with his disciples before his ascension. Since Jesus was in need of food after his tortuous death and burial experience, you can bet that he would work up an appetite explaining everything for more than a month. And if he ate, it's not too much of a leap to assume that he drank as well.

Whether Jesus drank wine or root beer during that time, the real convincer for me is what Jesus says right at the opening of the gospel of Mark:

> Now after John was arrested, Jesus came to Galilee, proclaiming the good news of God, and saying, "The time is fulfilled, and the kingdom of God has come near; repent, and believe in the good news." (Mark 1:14–15)

All three synoptics later tell a story of Jesus casting out some demons and the religious leaders accuse him of doing that by the power of Satan. Jesus challenges them in all three accounts, but Luke (and also Matthew) adds the clincher:

> But if it is by the finger of God that I cast out the demons, then the kingdom of God has come to you. (Luke 11:20)

It appears that Jesus was letting people know that the kingdom of God wasn't some pie-in-the-sky deal but was rather a present reality, bounding right into the midst of the drama of the human race. At the same time, there is an overriding expectation that this kingdom will come to a big-bang fulfillment at some point in the future. In the meantime, we followers of Jesus continue to live out kingdom realities in our communities of faith and in our engagement with the world around us.

The Eucharist gives me a picture of that enactment. We gather together at a table of remembering, eating meagerly and gingerly, sometimes with liturgical precision and other times with casual neglect. Yet, in all ways, the meal we share is but a shadow of the reality yet to come. We enact that meal, proclaiming the Lord's death until he comes, offering sign and wonder pointing to our future hope.

The Lord's Supper not only gives us an arena for proclaiming the Lord's death, but it also gives us the occasion to proclaim the reality of the kingdom of God—God's rule and reign that breaks through all the brokenness, superficiality, and pain of human life. And sometimes that occasion comes in ways that surprise us.

A couple of years ago Emily and I decided to take a wedding anniversary trip to a place we had never been: Las Vegas. I have lived in southern California my entire life and, except to pass through once on my way to somewhere else, I had never been to Las Vegas, which is only a four-hour drive. The town simply does not connect for me. I have no interest in gambling and the never-ending nightlife offers no appeal, since I find the night a very convenient time for sleeping.

We chose to drive there, however, in order to see the Cirque du Soleil show, *Beatles Love.*

Emily and I are both fans of the Beatles and have been since their arrival in the US in 1964. I was just entering the netherworld of male puberty when I was imprinted with this music and it has been echoing in my brain ever since. I think that if someone were to do a study about the kind of music you listen to when puberty hits it would be discovered that the music forms your appreciation for a certain type of music for the rest of your life. That's my theory.

We arrived at the hotel in the afternoon and decided to walk around the Strip for awhile. It was December and the Nevada desert was sparkly and chilled. I marveled at the garish architecture[1] and tried to steer clear of the street hawkers attempting to hand us invitations to strip clubs. Then we had a very nice dinner and entered the theater, where we ran into one of my students and his wife.[2]

The show was delightful and clearly worth our time and money. We then stood outside with all the other tourists and watched the fake volcano spew water all over the place, forcing us all to clap our hands as if we'd never seen such a thing.

The next morning we had breakfast and then walked through the casino part of the hotel as we prepared to head for home. As we strolled along the curving, carpeted pathway that drew us through the aisles of slot machines, I heard music playing over the hotel speakers. Holiday music had been playing at the hotel constantly since our arrival. It was the culturally-correct stuff that you often hear—fun, but having little to do with Christmas. My eyes were taking in the images of early morning gamblers staring at the lights and flashes of the machines, some with drinks from the bar at their elbows, when I stopped in my tracks. The music was different now and the difference hit me like rock. Rather than hearing Mel Torme or Bing Crosby, I heard a choir, and these were the words I could make out:

1. Which is like what I imagine Disneyland would look to you after you dropped acid.

2. And this is exactly why the maxim, "What happens in Vegas stays in Vegas" does not apply to people like us, because God will rat us out.

He rules the world with truth and grace
And makes the nations prove
The glory of his righteousness
And wonders of his love

It was *Joy to the World*,[3] but with a boldness that I had never heard before. It was a proclamation of the kingdom of God, not coming from a small band of the faithful out in the street, but right in the middle of a casino. The good news that God is king resonated through the building, and I may have been the only one to hear it.

I looked again at the floor of the casino. There is was: The place of empty promises and broken dreams. And into the midst of that false reality came the proclamation of the only thing that is real—the kingdom of God.

How amazing that the good news that Jesus proclaimed and lived out would come to us as invitation to his table. How amazing that, just for a few moments, voices would call out to the bleary-eyed Las Vegas gamblers that a new reality was theirs for the receiving. I wondered: Who were the people in the casino who were being called through this song? Surely there were just everyday people off on an excursion, but there might also be a pickpocket or two and maybe some prostitutes. There might be people who had lost it all and were dumping their last dollars into the machines that they prayed would change their lives. The music went out to them all.

While I didn't hear it, there is a verse that precedes this one:

No more let sins and sorrows grow,
Nor thorns infest the ground;
He comes to make his blessings flow
Far as the curse is found . . .

Sins—the many ways that we humans forget about God—and sorrows—the consequence of believing that God has forgotten us—are, we hear, no longer allowed to grow. Jesus has come to bring blessing to the world and the song was sung that December morning in a Vegas hotel casino. I wonder if someone else took notice. I wonder if someone got up from a slot machine, looked around, and headed outside to find the wonders of God's love. I don't know.

But I know that I heard it. And I believed it.

3. Watts. *Joy to the World.*

30

Pirate Communion

I CO-TEACH A COURSE for seminary students that focuses on preparation for ministry. We talk about the importance of having an inner life with God and also about how we engage with others in ministry. My friend and co-teacher is deeply committed to the care and formation of people's lives of faith and I love teaching with him. Our students generally report that the course has been helpful to them.

In the twenty weeks of the course a unique sense of community is created. We have the students tell their stories of faith and struggle and we teach them how to listen and pray for one another.[1] They spend time in small groups talking and praying together. They become connected in ways that deepen their learning experiences. Some even take the things we teach them and bring them into the lives of the people they lead and the churches in which they are involved.

Part of the course assignment is the requirement to work together to plan and participate in a five-hour retreat. Historically the course, when taught elsewhere, required the students to do the retreat on an individual basis, which was, in my view, an invitation for students to lie about really doing the retreat. Seminarians should avoid lying as part of their theological curriculum. I'm pretty sure of that.

To avoid encouraging the sin of lying, we made the retreat a communal activity. We divide the retreat into three components: Worship, a common meal, and Eucharist. We create three teams and every student is involved in the process. This is always fascinating to watch because our

1. Yes, seminary students have to be taught these things. You would think that folks involved in the work of leadership in churches would be good at things like listening and prayer, but they are too often taught to focus on the functional workings of church life. And it's not that my friend and I are so great at those things either. It's just that we've been around a long time and have learned our lessons the hard way.

students come from a variety of faith traditions and their preferences, especially for worship and Eucharist, bounce off of one another. Somehow, they always come up with something that pleases everyone.

We do this retreat on the last night of our class and we do it at my home. We have enough space inside and out to do this and it's a great way to deepen the learning and community experience. I really enjoy this time together because I am mostly an extrovert and get energized by people. My wife, on the other hand, is an introvert, and having fifteen or twenty strangers descend on her home gives her the willies. The cleanup on both sides of the event is enough to make her not speak to me for up to three days.

So you can imagine my concern when the first retreatants made a plan to share the Lord's Supper on my living room carpet with gallons of grape juice. When the Eucharist part of the evening came, the students produced pewter tankards and heavy glass chalices, one for each person in attendance. The plan was for each cup to be filled and for one person at a time to call out some word of praise or blessing to God. Then the group would cry out in unison, "Hallelujah, Amen!" To be honest, I thought the whole thing was a bit corny, but that's what happens when you turn people loose with something important.

As the jugs of grape juice were passed around the room and poured sloshingly into the cups, my life began to pass before my eyes. I imagined the people leaving and me standing in the room, counting the purple stains on the carpet. I envisioned the look on Emily's face as I tried to explain why I thought this was a good idea. I considered hopping a train and riding a box car to Hoboken.

The student who had come up with this idea started things rolling. "God is great!" he cried, lustily. Everyone crashed their tankards together, laughing and shouting, "Hallelujah, Amen!" We all guzzled simultaneously, the sweet sugar of the juice coursing through our veins.

I turned to the woman next to me and declared, "This is how pirates would do communion! Arrgghhh!"

"Arrgghhh!" she replied, clunking glass against pewter.

I watched for oversplash. It crossed my mind that it was a good thing we weren't using real wine for our Eucharistic hoe-down. Sending twenty people from my home to drive their cars after consuming five or six goblets of wine would have been irresponsible, not to mention disastrous for my career.

I was initially concerned that we were turning the Lord's Supper into something trivial, when a subtle shift occurred in the room. As each successive person called out a word of blessing and as the responses bounced off the walls, an atmosphere of worshipful celebration emerged. In all the set up and preparations for a unique and clever communion event, none of us noticed, until it was too late, that we were on holy ground.

None of us could quite explain what happened that evening, but we all agreed that something changed for us in the Eucharist. There we were—Presbyterians, Episcopalians, Pentecostals, Lutherans, and a mix of non-denominationalists—coming together in a Eucharistic experience that began as uncharted territory and ended up immersed in the presence of Jesus. We thought we had created our own particular kind of table, but it turned out to be a fresh aspect of the table that Jesus had already prepared for us.

Since that time there have been a few students in subsequent classes who, because of the requirements of their particular faith traditions, could not participate in our creative Eucharistic celebrations. We're fine with that, but we still embrace them and pull out a chair for them at the table. If they aren't able to eat and drink that night because of their consciences, we honor them by praying a word of blessing over them. In our celebrations, no one is turned away.

And I was not turned away from my home after our bohemian Eucharist. After all that pouring, clunking, and sloshing, not one drop of grape juice hit the floor. That was a miracle in itself. However, it took a couple of days for the sugar buzz to die down, which beats a hangover any day.

31

Places at the Table

My grandchildren provide me with rich material. They amaze me with their depth of thinking and their knack for comedy. That's a good combination, in my view.

Jacob, my oldest grandson, was the first to explore theology with me. When he was four, he spent the night with my wife and me for the first time. Jacob had been diagnosed with type-1 diabetes a year earlier and this was his first overnight venture in our care. He was bouncing with excitement and had specific plans for how our time together would be. As we sat down at the dinner table together, he set the stage for an important theological conversation.

"Let's talk, Grampa."

"Okay," I replied. "What do you want to talk about?"

"Let's talk about God," he said.

"Hmmm," I hummed. "What about God?"

"I know everything about God," he declared, offering me a look of bold confidence.

"Like what, Jacob?"

"Like, God made everything and I know everything that God made."

As a good grandfather, I think that my grandchildren are brilliant and don't mind telling that to everyone. On this night, however, I suspected that Jacob had overreached his grasp.

"What do you mean, Jacob?"

"Well, God didn't make chairs or cars or houses or tables. But God did make people, and dogs, and trees and water." He smiled at me victoriously.

I thought this was pretty good for a little kid. He had differentiated between the concepts of creation and re-creation. He understood that the things of the natural world came by the hand of God and that the things of our technological manipulations were part of our utilization of what God had created. I was proud of Jacob. I was pleased in seeing the evidence of my DNA in him.

He then scrunched his face in a conspiratorial way and leaned in close to me.

"And, Grampa, do you know who made God?" My concern light moved from green to yellow.

"No, who made God, Jacob?"

"The devil," he replied. I shuddered at the possible toxic nature of my DNA.

"I don't think that's right, Jacob."

"Oh, yes it is," he insisted. "My dad told me."

I was sure that my son-in-law had said no such thing, although I was tempted to shift the blame to his gene pool. Jacob and I talked through the various issues of good and evil and he became comfortable with God's eternal presence and the devil's inability to create anything except mischief.

Another grandson, Jacob's cousin Jude, has recently turned four and is now launching into this own theological reflections.[1] He has been having nightmares lately and is trying to find out where God is in this troubling place. My daughter and her husband have been giving Jude an early sense of faith and, true to form, he is taking it very seriously. Just this week he asked my daughter why God—the God who is supposed to be so good—would give him bad dreams. Let's face it: If God is the source of all things, then he must be the source of Jude's scary dreams.

It's tough to beat the logic in that. Such thinking about how there can be a good and benevolent God in a world of evil is called *theodicy*. As a late bloomer, I didn't learn this word until just a few years ago. My grandsons wrestle with the issue before kindergarten.[2]

My daughter tried to gently explain in four-year-old terms, about good and evil and what the Bible says about Satan. She was very cautious on this last point, taking care not to create a Star Wars dualism between

1. I think there is something about turning four years old that causes the males in my family to take risks in behavior and thinking. At four, my grandsons began exploring theology; at that same age, I peed on my neighbor's car. I think these might be developmental leaps.

2. I have photographs of my grandchildren, if you'd ever like to see them.

God and Satan, or to suggest that Satan was the monster living under Jude's bed. That wouldn't help the nightmare situation at all, nor would it assist in his development as a budding theologian.

Never one to leave a topic unexplored, Jude wanted to know whether or not God would forgive Satan for being evil if Satan said he was sorry. Maybe God could give Satan a "time out" and then let him back into the family, right? My daughter thought there was some merit in that possibility.

Theological arguments seem quite powerful in seminary classrooms or in discussion groups. They seem very fragile when four-year-olds start pumping you with questions and won't let you off the hook just because you know some big words. Maybe theological exams should conclude in preschools, where seminarians are left to the analytical devices of young children.

It is interesting to me how we find these young skeptics cute and adorable, but consider them troublesome and irritating when they enter adulthood. We have plenty of mini-chairs for our children with their misgivings about God, but the chairs for our adult doubters are often conspicuously roped off. Jesus had room at his table for doubters, cowards, and traitors. We sometimes only make room for the ones who agree with us.

I understand this difficulty because it's hard to eat and debate at the same time. Such a combination of activities is sure to produce indigestion and can take the ease and comfort out of a meal. But maybe our meal at the Lord's table isn't meant for ease and comfort. If the precedent of Scripture is any indicator, then the table of Jesus draws a motley crew of people who bring all their baggage with them. But when we take our seats, side by side, the backpacks and suitcases have to sit somewhere behind us. With the bounty of food and drink being served, there isn't room to put our stuff on the table. We can only bring ourselves.

I also understand the functional nature of churches. Churches are about *doing* things: Worship services, youth programs, weddings, funerals, discipleship classes, soup kitchens and so on. These are all good things but they need people to do them and we find it easier to do all these things with people who see eye-to-eye with us. I wonder if a fresh expression of the Eucharist can help us with this.

Jesus invited doubters and other broken creatures to his table. We need to think about the implications of our exclusion of those kinds of people.

There was a pub near my church office where I had lunch at least once a week. I made a commitment to that place and made it, so to speak, part of my parish. I learned the names of the workers and began to pray for them. Over time, some of them trusted me and used my weekly visit as a time to share bits and pieces of their lives. I kept this habit up for a number of years and became a part of this little pub community.

The bartender (a recovered alcoholic and metaphysical inquirer) and I became friends and met together regularly for breakfast. I enjoyed his friendship and the richness of our conversations. He and I generated an idea: What if we invited some of his co-workers into a little discussion group and called it the Big Questions group. We would talk together about the questions of life that vexed us and see where the conversation would take us. Two of the waitresses said they'd like to join in, and the BQ group was formed.

For three months these folks came to my house each week for dinner and conversation. The sky was the limit and I encouraged them to set the agenda for the discussion. We talked about relationships, fear, God and any number of other topics. Each week the openness and honesty increased and we shared the deeper and sometimes hidden parts of our lives.

One told of her father's AIDS-related death when she was sixteen years old. Another spoke of his mother's Roman Catholic-charismatic faith that caused him to be angry and now guilt-ridden since her recent death. The other began to wonder why her parents never spoke to her about God. We covered the dinner table with a paper table cloth that turned into a communal journal as we made notes of the parts of the conversation that were meaningful to us. After dinner, we cut up the cloth with scissors and everyone took their piece home. I later officiated at the wedding of the young woman who had confronted her parents regarding their silence about God. The parents avoided me at the wedding.

I count those evenings with my friends as one of the richest experiences of my life. We started out with me thinking about them as my new project—after all, I was a pastor and they were heathen pub-people. But we became a community bound to one another in love. We shared a weekly meal together and received one another as a temporary family. I fell in love with these people and soon came to realize that I was one of them. There was a holiness to that simple meal we shared. It smelled of Eucharist, a table set by Jesus and populated by those who responded to his invitation. The doubts, pain, and questions ran deep, but our time at the table bound us together as one body.

There are many places at the table of Jesus.

32

The Eucharistic Shape of Mission

I KNOW OF CHURCHES that invite non-believers into their works of service. These folks join in when the church feeds the poor and homeless or when they fix up a house for a family in a needy situation. These non-believing helpers might not attend a service, but they find meaning and purpose in helping others. Is that engagement in a common mission—a mission we believe comes at the summons of Jesus—a sufficient basis for coming to the common table?

Jesus said some scary words about his place among the needy as he spoke of the time of judgment at the end of the ages:

> Then the king will say to those at his right hand, "Come, you that are blessed by my Father, inherit the kingdom prepared for you from the foundation of the world; for I was hungry and you gave me food, I was thirsty and you gave me something to drink, I was a stranger and you welcomed me, I was naked and you gave me clothing, I was sick and you took care of me, I was in prison and you visited me." Then the righteous will answer him, "Lord, when was it that we saw you hungry and gave you food, or thirsty and gave you something to drink? And when was it that we saw you a stranger and welcomed you, or naked and gave you clothing? And when was it that we saw you sick or in prison and visited you?" And the king will answer them, "Truly I tell you, just as you did it to one of the least of these who are members of my family, you did it to me." (Matthew 25:34–40)

Jesus calls to us from the side of the world. When we come together with our hash of beliefs and questions, are we responding to the call of Jesus to be his people for the benefit and blessing of the world, or are we responding to a call to have our act together? Perhaps our difficulty with this is that we struggle with the idea of mission in the first place. But if mission—the mission of God's reconciling work in the world—is what we *are* rather than what we *do*, then perhaps we might be able to learn how to move between the work of God and the table of Jesus more fluidly, not allowing our doubts and questions to hinder our common life.

Our assistance mission to Louisiana after Hurricane Katrina in 2005 taught me something about Eucharist and mission.

Just a few days after the storm devastated the Gulf Coast, I was on my way to the dentist when my cell phone rang. It was my friend and fellow pastor, Floyd. He got right to the point.

"You know about Hurricane Katrina, right?" I affirmed that I occasionally listened to the news.

"Well," he said, "we need to quit just talking about doing the right thing and actually do something. We need to go to Louisiana and help."

"What do you mean *we*?" I asked.

"I mean you, me, and Steve," he said. Steve, Floyd, and I were all pastors and also good friends.

I did a quick mental calculation. "Floyd, our combined age is 160 years. We will die if we go there."

"It doesn't matter," he said. "We need to go."

"I'm going to the dentist," I said. "I'll call you later."

Certain that Floyd had flipped a cog, I went on to my appointment. As usual, my dentist, a fine Presbyterian, asked me what was new. Through a mouthful of dental devices and stuffings, I mumbled about my phone conversation with Floyd, assuming that my dentist would find it mildly amusing. When he heard my story, he stopped working on me and sat silently for a few seconds.

"I have 144 toothbrushes that I'll give you," he said. "And toothpaste, too."

I disliked his inability to laugh this situation off but figured I could pass the stuff off to Floyd and he could take it to his doom. I left my dental appointment with boxes of toothbrushes and toothpaste. I called my wife to tell her what had happened. She began to cry, which was not a good sign.

"I think you need to go," she sniffled. I hate it when she does this, because I'm pretty sure that God likes her better than he does me and she probably has a direct line to him.

This took place on a Thursday. By Sunday morning we were driving to Baton Rouge with a team of eight people, four vehicles filled with supplies, and $20,000.00 of donations.[1] I wondered where they would bury me. I imagined setting up camp in a rain-soaked parking lot of the storefront church that would be hosting us. Instead, we arrived in Baton Rouge two days later to find a beautiful little church resting on seventeen wooded acres. I considered the possibility that church life in Louisiana was different than what I experienced in southern California. We set up camp and took our daily assignments.

Each day we would head out to work. Some would deliver or pick up pallets of supplies; others would go into homes and schools, tearing out rotted carpet and moldy drywall. We took time to pray for people when we could. The days were filled with heavy labor but also with a richness of ministry that was profound. At the end of the day we regrouped at our campsite to share a simple meal together.[2]

There was a simple rhythm to our days. We gathered with the other pilgrims for early morning worship, then journeyed down the road to help people in need. In the evening we returned home to a table set that would nourish and refresh us, giving us space to tell the stories of our day. We developed a deep sense of community that gave a new expression to our common life in the church that identifies itself with Jesus.

At the end of a church service, many churches charge the people to return to the outside world, "to love and serve the Lord." My time on the Gulf Coast gave me a sense of that fluid life of worship, Eucharist, and mission. We did it every day during our time there. I wonder what happens to us when we engage together only once a month or once a quarter or once a year or so?

I used to agree with those who claimed that they didn't need to go to church in order to be Christians. Now, I'm not really sure that I believe that anymore.

1. My bartender friend's brother sent us an additional $10,000. He did not claim to be a follower of Jesus, but just wanted to help.

2. Upon our arrival in Baton Rouge we discovered that the local Winn-Dixie was fully supplied and had an impressive selection of wines. We might have been eating canned beef stew for dinner, but it went down easy with a glass or two of Cabernet Sauvignon. We were living simply, but that didn't mean we were barbarians.

33

Rules of Engagement

I AM AWARE THAT the various faith traditions often have particular requirements for those who partake in the Lord's Supper during a worship service. Some require Christian baptism; others ask that a person be a baptized Christian and a member of that particular faith community or tradition. Still others want to make sure that a person has made a personal commitment to Jesus. What is required to come to the Lord's table is not a topic upon which we all agree.

It occurs to me that there were no Christians at the last supper. Everyone at the table, including Jesus, was Jewish. There was among them no concept of a religion known as Christianity or of an individualized faith expression so common among people like us. The gathered disciples might have agreed, to an extent, that Jesus was the long-awaited Jewish messiah, but that didn't necessarily translate into Jesus as the third person of the Trinity or as the Son of God.[1] When it came to a common understanding during that inaugural meal, the boys from Galilee were all over the map.

Even the level of belief around that first table was questionable. Not a one of them believed in the resurrection, because it hadn't yet occurred. Even after that event, Thomas wouldn't buy in without tangible proof. Peter would duck and run in a few hours and Judas was already about the business of betrayal. Jesus passed the bread and cup to all of them and promised to join them in this meal again someday.

How did we move from this original sloppy, eclectic gathering to one outlined by specific rules of engagement in the ways we practice today? What is the preference of Jesus when it comes to his table?

1. See footnote 20.

While held at Tegel military prison in 1945 prior to his execution, Dietrich Bonhoeffer served as a pastor to his fellow inmates. While many of his fellow prisoners were German Lutherans, one member of this prison community stood outside of that national and religious heritage. This one was a Russian, and held no religious views except that of atheism. It appears, however, that their solidarity as captives of the Nazis drew the prisoners together in ways that transcended the old familiar boundaries.

The Lutheran prisoners asked Bonhoeffer to lead them in a celebration of the Lord's Supper and he was happy to oblige. The Russian, however, excused himself from the service, refusing its religious expression but also respecting the beliefs of his comrades. Bonhoeffer would not accept the man's declination. He insisted that if all would not partake, then none would partake. In the end, the Russian took his seat at the table of Jesus.[2]

Bonhoeffer was an ordained Lutheran minister, so I'm sure he knew the appropriate limitations regarding the Eucharist. Things changed, however, when human beings who were considered categorically abstract became relationally concrete. When we look into one another's eyes we not only see a real person but we also see the reflection of ourselves. In mutual relationship we enter into solidarity with one another and the walls that have separated us begin to crumble.

When I was in my mid-twenties I was struggling with my own sense of identity and purpose.[3] After taking a couple of undergraduate psychology courses I became a psychological expert and came to the conclusion that it was my father's fault that I had issues (this is what we first-born sons do—we always blame our fathers and then we become one). I came to the brilliant conclusion that my dad wasn't perfect, therefore he was responsible for whatever it was that ailed me.

One weekend he and I had the occasion to take a casual walk together. While we strolled, he told me a couple of stories of his life that I had never heard before.[4] He told me that when he was two years old, he was shipped

2. "They were a mixed group of Protestants and Catholics, but that hardly mattered any more. They had lived through such times a made Confessional differences peripheral. There was only one difficulty—Wasiliew Kokorin. He was an atheist and a loyal communist. Bonhoeffer could not tolerate the thought that any of their number be separated from them at such a service. Although he must have longed to conduct the service he refused because their solidarity was more important than a religious service. It was only when Kokorin asked him and wanted to be included that he agreed." Robertson, *The Shame and the Sacrifice*, 275).

3. One of many to come, of course.

4. My dad is clearly one of the best story-tellers around.

off to live with his grandparents. He didn't know why this happened, but we both guessed that his parents were struggling during the effects of the depression and needed a kid-free environment for a while. My dad was the only child at the time, but maybe he was a handful.

When Dad was four years old, my grandparents took him back home and introduced him to his new, two-year-old brother. Things did not go well between them, since each one thought he was the only child in the family. I loved my paternal grandparents, but their neglecting to tell siblings about each other's existence ranked right at the top of the stupid list as far as I was concerned. How this could happen still boggles my mind.

The other story took place when he was in the army during the Second World War. He was stationed at the time in New Jersey, awaiting orders to go overseas. He had some time off so he decided to hitch a ride to his family home in Nebraska. Upon his arrival, he was shocked to discover that his parents' home was empty. He checked in with a neighbor and learned that the family had moved to the state of Washington, but forgot to tell my dad. I made another entry on the stupid list.[5]

When my dad told me these stories, I saw him differently. Here was a child and a young man, trying to find his way in the world and getting precious little help in doing it. At least twice he was cast adrift from his family and had to make the best of it. Out of those kinds of experiences he should have turned out to be a dismal character. Instead, he turned out to be my dad, and a pretty good one at that. I had cast my father into an abstact category and thought that I could stand away from him, analyze him, and even enter into a place of judgment against him. But in the gift of mutual relationship, I could not enjoy that place of self-appointed objectivity. I now entered into solidarity with someone who was just like me in many ways.

At the table of Jesus, we come not out of individually attained qualification, but instead as co-humans, made in the image of God and invited universally to receive the invitation given graciously to us. If we try to come to the table for any other reason than that, then the bread will be stale and the wine bitter. If we come because we are qualified and others are not, then we come out of false pretense. It is Jesus who does the inviting, not me.

5. I have seen some of the letters my grandmother wrote to my dad when he was in the army. They were warm and chatty, the kind of letters you would expect a mother to write to a son. I suspect that my grandparents were as clueless about doing life as the next person and were stumbling to find their way along.

34

Looking for Jesus at the Table

THE APOSTLE'S QUOTATION STILL echoes off the walls of our churches daily, weekly and monthly:

> "Do this, as often as you drink it, in remembrance of me."
> (I Corinthians 11:25)

These, we are told, are the words of Jesus. Where have I found *this* in the Eucharist? I began writing as one confessing his inability to connect with the *this* of the Lord's Supper. No matter how hard I try, I cannot find the literal body and blood of Jesus in those temporal elements. Even when I squint my eyes tightly and search my poor, dark heart, I am at a loss to find Jesus hidden somewhere, even spiritually, in the bread and wine. And the purely symbolic nature of the whole thing leaves me wondering about its necessity.

Perhaps I have been looking in the wrong places.

I wonder if part of my own struggle in finding meaning in the Eucharist comes out of a struggle with seeing God in anything material. I don't know if this is a problem or not, but it seems to be the way I view the world.

Many years ago, during a time of retreat in the mountains, my friend and I took a walk through the woods and came to a spot that offered a wonderful view of the local scenery. He began to verbalize, quite loudly, praises to God for the beauty all around him. I didn't get very excited about that connection, even though I thought the view was very nice.

I've been to some truly beautiful places in the world, but I have rarely, if ever, looked at the natural beauty before me and marveled at what God has made. I just don't respond that way. But I have learned to marvel at something else: That I marvel in the first place. I find it extraordinary that I have a capacity for wonder and an appreciation for beauty. When I am in the eastern Sierras, I look at the pristine lakes and the exotic Minarets and feel something within me long to drink in the beauty, as if I were made to live and die in the uncontrived beauty of the world.[1] I find a different and deeper sense of being human in those places than I do in the city.

I think that my journey through the Eucharist requires me to quit trying to see Jesus in bread and wine and, instead, start allowing myself to marvel at the deep, mysterious love of God that comes to me in the face and voice of Jesus, inviting me to come to the table and wonder.

Soon after Mother Teresa's death, the release of her private letters was big news. This courageous woman of faith and love who served the destitute and marginalized of Calcutta, this woman who claimed to encounter Jesus among the poor, confessed that she had lived in a dark night of the soul for over fifty years. The young nun who, before embarking on her mission, would worship deeply and passionately within her Roman Catholic tradition, now found herself living out what she believed was God's destiny for her and doing so with an emptiness of heart.

How does such a thing happen? How does a faithful person embrace this world-impacting mission out of obedience to and love for God, only to find him absent to her for the rest of her life? Some suggest that this was God's test of faithfulness for her. Skeptics say that she had no God in the first place and did her charitable work within an illusory worldview. Other supporters say that Christ was, of course, with her whether she perceived him or not.

I wonder if Mother Teresa was looking for Jesus in the wrong places. In the cloister, she experienced God in the familiar rituals and patterns of a shared life of faith. But in the crucible of her call, her encounters with God would now be different. Perhaps the deeper structure of worship would be found in her ministry to the broken. Maybe she would no longer see Jesus in the carvings of the crucifix because she was encountering him in the contours of human life. It might be that she continued to look for Jesus in the familiar places, not realizing that he was summoning her from those ravaged, dark corners where he lived among the destitute.

1. I recognize immediately that to say this also creates the possibility that my death could take place in the embrace of a grizzly bear, which would probably alter my view of natural beauty.

There is a possibility that Mother Teresa didn't give her expectations permission to change locations.

I am speculating, of course. But this is helping me to recognize that my own dark day of the Eucharist might have sprung from my limited vision. I am coming to realize that I am discovering Jesus not so much in the elements themselves, but at the table of invitation. When I look into the eyes of those who share the meal with me, I see not only reflections of myself, but also the image of God with us. I count the people at the table and I know there is always an additional presence in the room. When I stand shoulder to shoulder with those who are not me but are very much like me, I know that we come to the table together, universally invited and welcomed by the one who has made it all possible. In that understanding I lose my sense of qualification or disqualification and superiority or inferiority and rest in the miracle that any of us have been invited to the table in the first place. I abandon my hope for worthiness because I have been invited by the only one who is truly worthy.

I find *this* in the presence of Jesus who, by the power of the Holy Spirit, remains among us.

I find *this* in the people who gather at the table, not to make a point or to jump through religious hoops, but to shed their sorrows and alienation and partake of the banquet feast set just for them.

I find *this* in the ones who carry doubts and skepticism, juggling their wish-dreams with faith, yet come wonderingly to the mystery that is the invitation to the table of Jesus.

I find *this* in those who come when self-absolution fails them and forgiveness remains elusive at best, and yet marvel when the meal is laid out for them, recognizing that their arrival was always anticipated.

I find *this* in the recognition that every Eucharistic meal is a preparation for the future that God intends, a future proclaimed and demonstrated by Jesus, and a future of God's intention where Jesus awaits us.

It is this Eucharist that feeds and nourishes me. It is not a Eucharist of abstraction but rather a meal of invitation and relationship.

And, miracle of all miracles, I have been invited to take, eat, and drink.

Bibliography

Anderson, Ray S. *The Soul of Ministry: Forming Leaders for God's People.* Louisville: Westminster John Knox, 1997.

Bonhoeffer, Dietrich. *Sanctorum Communio: A Theological Study of the Sociology of the Church.* Minneapolis: Fortress, 1998.

Lewis, C. S. *The Last Battle.* New York: HarperCollins, 2000.

Luther, Martin. "Sermons on the First Epistle of St. Peter." Vol. 30 of *Luther's Works*, edited by Jaroslav Pelikan. St. Louis: Concordia, 1967.

Neuhaus, Richard John. *Death on a Friday Afternoon.* New York: Basic Books, 2000.

Newbigin, Lesslie. *The Open Secret: An Introduction to the Theology of Mission.* Grand Rapid, MI: Wm. B. Eerdmans, 1995.

Parker, T. H. L. *John Calvin: A Biography.* Louisville: Westminster John Knox, 2006.

Robertson, Edwin. *The Shame and the Sacrifice.* London: Hodder and Stoughton, 1987.

Watts, Isaac. "Joy to the World." 1719.

Wright, N. T. *Simply Christian: Why Christianity Makes Sense.* San Francisco: HarperCollins, 2006.

Made in the USA
Lexington, KY
04 January 2016